George Hoadly

Before the Commission Created by Act of Congress,

Approved January 29, 1877

In the matter of the electoral votes of the states of Florida and Oregon

George Hoadly

Before the Commission Created by Act of Congress, Approved January 29, 1877
In the matter of the electoral votes of the states of Florida and Oregon

ISBN/EAN: 9783337038588

Printed in Europe, USA, Canada, Australia, Japan

Cover: Foto ©Suzi / pixelio.de

More available books at **www.hansebooks.com**

Before the Commission created by Act of Congress, approved
January 29, 1877,

IN THE MATTER

OF THE

ELECTORAL VOTES

OF THE

STATES OF FLORIDA AND OREGON.

ARGUMENTS OF

GEORGE HOADLY,

OF CINCINNATI, OHIO,

February 8 and 21, 1877.

" *Victrix causa Diis placuit, sed victa Catoni.*"

CINCINNATI:
ROBERT CLARKE & CO., PRINTERS.
1877.

IN THE MATTER

ELECTORAL VOTE OF THE STATE OF FLORIDA.

Upon the 8th of February, 1877, in the Supreme Court room, Mr. HOADLY *made the following argument upon the question of the disability of* FREDERICK C. HUMPHREYS *to cast one of the electoral votes of the State of Florida.*

MAY IT PLEASE THE COMMISSION:—It has been established by the proof that Frederick C. Humphreys held the office of shipping commissioner by appointment of the circuit court of the United States in Florida. It has been established by the proof that before the November election he attempted to divest himself of this office by forwarding to the city of Newark, in the State of Ohio, a paper resignation of that office, and by receiving from the judge, not the court, acting not in Florida but in Ohio, an acceptance of that resignation.

The powers of this office are derived from section 4501 of the Revised Statutes:

The several circuit courts within the jurisdiction of which there is a port of entry, etc., shall appoint, etc.

The resignation can not be made except to the same authority that appointed. The resignation could not, therefore, be made by letter addressed to the judge in Ohio. The acceptance of the resignation could not emanate from the judge in Ohio. The court has not since held a session. The court which clothed the officer with the power has not relieved him from the performance of the duty, and I respectfully submit that this proposition is sustained by the cause recently decided in the Supreme Court of the United States, the opinion in which has just been placed in my hands, the case of Badger and others v. The United States on the relation of Bolton, a copy of the decision in which will be furnished to your honors. It is also, I am advised, according to the practice of the Government, as shown by Document No. 123, Twenty-sixth Congress, second session, House of Representatives, and by the second volume of the Opinions of the Attorneys-General, pages 406 and 713. Therefore, considering that Frederick C. Humphreys had been duly appointed to this office, that by the laws of the United States it is shown to be an office of profit and trust, is by the Revised Statutes so made ; considering that the judge of the circuit court acting in Ohio was not the circuit court and was not the power that clothed him with the authority, and could not relieve him from the performance of the duty with which he had been intrusted by another power ; considering that the judge of the circuit court of the United States acting in chambers could not in Ohio release him from a trust with which the court not in chambers clothed him in Florida ; considering these circumstances, we respectfully submit that he held an office of profit and trust on the day of the November election for electors of President and Vice-President, and that therefore the vote that he cast as an elector in December can not be counted.

The provision of disqualification contained in the

first section of the second article of the Constitution I
will read, that I may have freshly before my own mind
the text in reference to which this debate must proceed.
There is nothing in the statute with regard to the resignation of this office at all. Having accepted the
office, given bond, and taken oath to perform its duties,
we submit that he could not divest himself of it by his
own act. I will read the whole section which authorized
the appointment :

> The several circuit courts within the jurisdiction of which there
> is a port of entry which is also a port of ocean navigation shall
> appoint a commissioner for each such port which in their judg-
> ment may require the same, such commissioners to be termed
> shipping commissioners ; and may, from time to time, remove
> from office any commissioner whom the court may have reason
> to believe does not properly perform his duties, and shall then
> provide for the proper performance of his duties until another per-
> son is duly appointed in his place.

I submit that where the legislative body have created
an office, and the judicial authority has, according to
the law, clothed a person with the trusts of that office,
public policy requires that it should not be held at his
will and pleasure, it being an office of public conveni-
ence and necessity, for the performance of which bond
is required to be given, and the filling of which may be
at all times essential to the performance of public duty.

Turning to the constitutional provision, I read :

> Each state shall appoint, in such manner as the Legislature
> thereof may direct, a number of electors equal to the whole num-
> ber of Senators and Representatives to which the State may be
> entitled in the Congress ; but no Senator or Representative, or
> person holding an office of trust or profit under the United States,
> shall be appointed an elector.

The form is mandatory ; it is negative ; that is,
the provision of disqualification is negative. It is

coupled with the grant of power by the word " but," which, together with the words of the context, shows that it is a limitation, a qualification, a diminution of the grant of power. The grant of power is to the State, not to the people of the State, but to the State as a legal entity, as an organized body, corporate in its character ; and to this grant thus given to the State is attached a limitation introduced by words of exception "*but* no Senator or Representative shall be entitled." It is clothed in negative language. "Negative language," it is said, "will make a statute imperative ; and this is incontestable. Negative words will make a statute imperative. Affirmative words may ; negative must," as is stated in Sedgwick on Constitutional and Statutory Law, page 370 ; and Cooley on Constitutional Limitations, 75 ; Potter's Dwarris on Statutes, 228 ; Rex *v.* Justices of Leicester, 7 Barnewall & Cresswell, 6, 12.

But what is of more consequence than the form, although the form is indicative of the purpose of the authors in using the words of substance, the provision is in substance imperative, and admits of no evasion. Lord Mansfield distinguishes mandatory from directory clauses in statutes by reference to " circumstances which are of the essence of a thing required to be done" as distinguished from circumstances which are " merely directory." Rex *v.* Loxdale, 1 Burr. 447.

Having relation, as Lord Mansfield says, to that which is essential as different from that which is merely directory, I suggest that several circumstances show that our fathers, who framed this provision, considered it essential. It seems to have been first adopted into the Constitution on the motion of Mr. Gerry and Mr. Gouverneur Morris, in a slightly different form from that in which it now appears. On July 19, 1787, Mr. Gerry and Mr. Gouverneur Morris moved " that the

electors of the Executive shall not be members of the
National Legislature, nor officers of the United States,
nor shall the electors themselves be eligible to the Supreme Magistracy. Agreed to *nem. con."* (*Madison
Papers*, 343.)

On September 6, Mr. Rufus King and Mr. Gerry
moved to insert in the fourth clause of the report, after
the words " may be entitled in the Legislature," the
following :

> But no person shall be appointed an elector who is a member
> of the Legislature of the United States, or who holds any office
> of profit or trust under the United States. *Madison Papers*,
> 515.

It passed *nem. con.* It was the unanimous will of
our fathers, therefore, that this disqualification should
attach ; that it should attach in the nature of an exception or proviso to the grant of powers to the States to
elect electors ; that it should attach by disqualification
of the persons who might be appointed electors ; that
it should attach by disqualification of the State in the
appointment of electors. The State is disqualified from
appointing, the elector from accepting the trust. The
disqualification, therefore, is imposed both upon the appointing power and upon the candidate, and the effect
of such disqualification, it is respectfully submitted, is
to render the action of the State in the appointment
null and void. The disqualification is of the action of
the State ; of the State in all its departments ; of the
voters of the State as well as of the government of the
State. The disqualification binds every citizen of the
State, every functionary of the State, and attaches to and
qualifies and limits the corporate action of the State,
and is equivalent to saying " the State may appoint
from among the number of qualified persons." I submit that the substance and real meaning of the sentence,

although it is cast in the negative and inhibitory form, is that from among the number of those who do not occupy positions of profit and trust the State may appoint electors. The object of our fathers in introducing, without dissent, this provision, was to prevent the Federal power, the officers controlling Federal agencies, from continuing their power through the influence of the offices of trust with which they were clothed for Federal and State benefit. It was not merely to protect the State in which the candidate might be elected from the intrusion of a Federal office-holder into the electoral office, but it was to protect every other State, each State, all the States, and the people of each and every State by a mutual covenant in the form of a limitation of power, that no State should appoint a disqualified person. Each State, therefore, through the agencies of the Federal Government, is entitled to be protected from the illegitimate use of Federal power in any State. Delaware, Oregon, the smallest of our States, are entitled to ask, through their Senators and Representatives, that the Federal power shall enforce this provision for their protection against the corruption of the elections in the larger States by means of the election of disqualified persons.

If it be said—but I do not think it will—that the remedy which our fathers provided for the evil which they apprehended has but little value, and that their forecast was not great, so much the more reason for rigidly insisting upon such value as it possesses now; for surely time has not proved, experience has not shown that the evils which our fathers apprehended, as they clearly manifested and showed by the text of the provision itself, are any less than they supposed they would be. The influence of Federal power through the candidacy of Federal officers for electors is explicitly here prohibited. The object is to diminish and prevent and restrict Federal interference in the election of electors. It is the duty, not of the States, in purging the votes of electors, but of the Federal Government, for the protection of each State, to insist upon and carry into full force this provision.

Again, the occasions upon which this provision has been considered during our history emphasize this suggestion as to the purpose of our fathers in adopting it. In 1837 five postmasters, or five persons bearing the same names as certain postmasters, were appointed or attempted to be appointed electors. Mr. Clay submitted, on January 27, 1837, this instruction, which he asked to be given to the joint committee of the Senate and House appointed to ascertain and report a mode of examining the votes for President and Vice-President of the United States, namely : that they should

"inquire into the expediency of ascertaining whether any votes were given at the recent election contrary to the prohibition contained in the second section of the second article of the Constitution ; and if any such votes were given, what ought to be done with them ; and whether any and what provision ought to be made for securing the faithful observance, in future, of that section of the Constitution."

The members of this committee on the part of the Senate were Felix Grundy, Henry Clay, and Silas Wright ; on the part of the House, Francis Thomas, Churchill C. Cambreleng, John Reed, Henry W. Connor, and Francis S. Lyon, the latter of whom, I was informed in Mobile a few days since, is the only survivor, now living in Alabama at a great age, and deeply interested in this discussion. Mr. Grundy submitted a report of the committee on February 4, from which I desire to read the following quotation :

That the short period at which they were appointed, before the day on which the votes for President and Vice-President of the United States have to be counted, has prevented them from investigating the facts submitted to their examination as fully as might have been done had more time been allowed. The correspondence which has taken place between the chairman of the committee and the heads of the different departments of the executive branch of the government accompanies this report, from which it appears . . . that in two cases persons of the same names with the individuals who were appointed and voted as electors in the State of North Carolina held the office of deputy-postmaster under the General Government.

I suggest, in passing, that the course taken by this committee of the most eminent men of that generation indicates that I am right in the suggestion that the duty was then considered, as we now claim it should be, as imposed on the Federal power to take testimony so as to ascertain the facts and by Federal agencies enforce the prohibition for the protection, not merely of the State in which the disqualified elector has voted, but of the States in which the disqualified elector has not voted for the election of President and Vice-President, and thus that it concerns all the States, and relates to the deepest and most vital interests of all the States. The disqualification can not therefore be permitted to be evaded in one State without a blow struck at every other State.

I will continue reading the report :

It also appears that in New Hampshire there is one case ; in Connecticut there is one case ; in North Carolina there is one case in which, from the report of the Postmaster-General, it is probable that at the time of the appointment of electors in these States respectively the electors or persons of the same name were deputy-postmasters. The committee have not ascertained whether the electors are the same individuals who held or are presumed to have held the office of deputy-postmasters at the time when the appointment of electors was made ; and this is the less to be regretted, as it is confidently believed that no change in the result of the election of either the President or Vice-President would be affected by the ascertainment of the fact in either way, as five or six votes only would, in any event, be abstracted from the whole number, for the committee can not adopt the opinion entertained by some, that a single illegal vote would vitiate the whole electoral vote of the college of electors in which it was given, particularly in cases where the vote of the whole college has been given for the same persons.

From this sentence it appears that at that time, forty years ago, the question in debate was whether the single illegal vote vitiated more than the vote itself, and the committee were of opinion that it did not.

The committee are of opinion that the second section of the second article of the Constitution, which declares that " no Senator or Representative, or person holding an office of trust or profit under the United States, shall be appointed an elector," ought to be carried, in its whole spirit, into rigid execution, in order to prevent officers of the General Government from bringing their official power to influence the elections of President and Vice-President of the United States. This provision of the Constitution, it is believed, excludes and disqualifies deputy-postmasters from the appointment of electors ; and the disqualification relates to the time of the appointments, and that a resignation of the office of deputy-postmaster after his appointment as elector would not entitle him to vote as elector under the Constitution.

I submit that when it appears that two such minds as those of Henry Clay and Silas Wright, statesmen of such opposite political education and modes of thought, concur in a statement with reference to the reasons and meaning of the Constitution, it comes to us with a weight and with an authority that is not to be gainsaid. Fortunately or unfortunately, however, our American habit of not bridging chasms until we reach them prevented any action by Congress such as Mr. Clay suggested ; and accordingly the question represents itself to-day without any further elucidation by legislation than it had then.

If we are right in our proposition with regard to the facts, Humphreys held the office at the time when he cast his vote. The only two questions, therefore, which present themselves for debate are, first, did he hold at the time an office of profit and trust; secondly, as to the effect of the holding, provided the fact has been shown. As the questions thus present themselves, we are not concerned to consider the authorities decided in cases of resignation after the election, except so far as they indicate the views of courts with regard to the effect of the disqualifying facts. In Rex *v.* Monday (Cowper, page 536), Sergeant Buller, afteward Mr. Justice Buller, states the rule thus, *arguendo:*

> Two requisites are necessary to make a good election: first, a capacity in the electors; second, a capacity in the elected; and unless both concur the election is a nullity. . . . With respect to the capacity of the electors, their right is this: They can not say there shall be no election, but they are to elect. Therefore, though they may vote to prefer one to fill an office, they can not say that such a one shall not be preferred, or by merely saying " We dissent to every one proposed," prevent any election at all. Their right consists in an affirmative, not a negative declaration. Consequently there is no effectual means of voting against one man but by voting for another; and even then, if such other person be unqualified and the elector has notice of his incapacity, his vote will be thrown away.

Such is the well-settled English rule, as affirmed by a multitude of cases since.

Lord Chief-Justice Wilmot, in the same volume, note to page 393, in the case of Harrison *v.* Evans, discussing the statute of 13 Charles II, which enacted that no person should be elected into any corporation-office who had not received the sacrament within a twelvemonth preceding his election, and in default of doing so the election and choice should be void, said:

> The provision is not only addressed to the elected and a provision upon them, but a provision laid down upon the electors

if they have notice. The Legislature has commanded them not
to choose a non-conformist, because he ought not to be trusted.
Consequently, with respect to any legal effect of operation, it
is as if there had been no election.

So in a multitude of cases in England since, as I
said, which need not be here more particularly referred
to, but with a reference to which your honors will be
furnished in my brief. The same doctrine is applied
in many American cases also, and it is respectfully submitted that there is no case to the contrary. American cases have differed widely upon the question
whether the non-eligibility of the candidate receiving
the largest vote has the effect to elect the next highest
competing candidate; but no American case, it is respectfully submitted, treats the election of one who at
the time was non-qualified and who attempted to act, as
other than an absolutely null appointment. To this
effect is the case of Searcy v. Grow, 15 California, 118,
which was a contest for the office of sheriff of Siskiyou
county, where Grow was returned as having been elected
and was found to be the holder of an office of profit
and trust under the constitution of California, to which
a disqualification was attached by the constitution, and
who had resigned after the election and before induction
into the shrievalty, but was holding the disqualifying
office at the time of the election. Mr. Justice Baldwin,
Cope, J., and Field, C. J., concurring, said :

The people in this case were clothed with this power of choice.
Their selection of a candidate gave him all the claim to the office
which he has. His title to the office comes from their designa-
tion of him as sheriff. But they could not designate or choose a
man not eligible—that is, not capable of being selected. They
might select any man they chose, subject only to this exception :
That the man they selected was capable of taking what they had
the power to give. We do not see how the fact that he became
capable of taking office after they had exercised their power can

avail the appellant. If he was not eligible at the time the votes were cast for him, the election failed.

Of course your honors will see the pertinency of this quotation to other questions that may arise in other cases, and I am compelled to read portions of the opinion which do not refer to the particular case in hand, in order to use intelligently those portions that do:

If he was not eligible at the time the votes were cast for him, the election failed. We do not see how it can be assumed that by the act of the candidate the votes which, when cast, were ineffectual because not given for a qualified candidate, became effectual to elect him to office.

So in the case of the State of Nevada on the relation of Nourse *v.* Clarke (3 *Nevada*, 566,) which, it is true, may be treated as *obiter dictum*, because it was found there that the resignation had been effectually made before the election, the court discussed this question with this result: " That a person holding the office of United States district attorney on the day of election was incapable of being chosen to the office of attorney-general of the State, because of a provision in the State constitution to the effect that no Federal office-holder ' shall be eligible to any civil office of profit under this State.' ' Which word eligible,' says this learned court, ' means both of being legally chosen and capable of legally holding.' "

The word here is " appointed;" that no person holding an office shall be *appointed* an elector. Who appoints? The State appoints; not the voters of the State; not the Legislature of the State; not the Governor of the State; but the State appoints. The State appoints from among qualified persons; or, which is the same thing, the State appoints, but may not appoint a disqualified person. Now, the State does appoint a disqualified person, and the disqualification is one contained in the same constitutional provision as a qualification, limitation, restriction of the same constitutional clause which gives the right to appoint, a part of the same sentence attached to the grant of power. The appointment refers to the act of the State, the act of the State on the day which Congress has named as the day upon which only the choice of elector can be made. On that day the State shall appoint, but shall not appoint a person not legally qualified to hold the office.

In Commonwealth *v*. Cluly (56 Pennsylvania State Reports, 270) the election went back to the people. In the Indiana cases the next highest competing candidate was declared elected—going beyond the rule we ask to be applied to the Florida electoral college. In Searcy *v*. Grow, I suppose the result of the contest was to unseat the disqualified person without seating the next highest competing candidate. In all the cases which are commented upon in the decision of Gulick *v*. New, in 14 Indiana, 93, and by the various authorities and text-writers on this subject, no one, I submit, will be found which favors the idea that the election of one constitutionally disqualified can by any possibility result, if it do not elect the next highest candidate, in anything else than a failure to elect; and Congress by its legislation on the subject has indicated its purpose in the same direction. Thus the one hundred and thirty-third section of the Revised Statutes provides for a case of vacancy occurring when the college of electors shall meet to cast their votes. Section 134 provides for a case where the State shall fail to elect; that, where the State shall fail to elect on the day provided, the electors may be appointed on a subsequent day in such manner as the Legislature of such State may direct. These provisions of law, which have been in force since the act of January 23, 1845, in that statute were attached, and not separated as in the Revised Statutes and thrown into two separate sections; these two provisions of law, which were then attached to each other, indicate the meaning of the law-makers of this generation and the last to furnish a remedy in case of the election of one disqualified under the Constitution.

If it be shown that the State of Florida has acted under the one hundred and thirty-fourth section of the Revised Statutes, then the vote of Florida is not diminished by reason of the fact that on the 7th of November one of the persons voted for was disqualified.

Sec. 134. Whenever any State has held an election for the purpose of choosing electors, and has failed to make a choice on the day prescribed by law, the electors may be appointed on a subsequent day in such a manner as the Legislature of such State may direct.

If it were true, as ruled in Furman v. Clute, 50 New York Reports; in Commonwealth v. Cluly, 56 Pennsylvania State Reports; in Searcy v. Grow, in 15 California Reports; if it were true, as ruled in all the American cases, which have held that the next highest competing candidate was not elected, that the case was one of non-election, and rendered necessary a new election, then I respectfully submit that the one hundred and thirty-fourth section of the Revised Statutes provided for the State of Florida a remedy for the mischief to which she was found on the 7th of November to have been subjected. She could have provided by law, as I shall presently show to your honors was done in the State of Rhode Island, to meet the exact contingency. It is not the case of an absolute non-election, or one where there has been no attempt to hold an election to which this section refers. This provision

of law operates whenever any State has held an election
for the purpose of choosing electors and has failed to
make a choice on the day prescribed by law. Then the
electors may be appointed on a subsequent day in such
manner as the Legislature of such State may direct.

If every elector in every State in the United States
were disqualified, would it not be true that there was an
election held and a failure to make choice? If every
elector in the State of Florida was disqualified, would
it not be true that there was an election held, but
without choice? If, in the State of Pennsylvania,
in the case of Cluly, the people had again to elect ; if,
in New York, in Furman v. Clute, the people had again
to elect ; if, in California, in the case of Searcy v. Grow,
the people had again to elect, then it would follow that,
if all the four electors of the State of Florida were disqualified, it would be clearly a case of failure to make
choice, and the people would have to elect again, provided the Legislature confided to the people, under section 134, the function of electing for the second time
and did not exercise it themselves, as was done in
Rhode Island. *Omne majus continet in se minus.*

If it be a failure to make choice where a single disqualified candidate runs against another officer, if it
be a failure to make choice so that he can be ousted
and a new election is required to be held, and if there
be a provision of statute law of the United States con-
templating the emergency and providing a remedy, and
if the power of appointment be with the State, and if
the opportunity of remedy be with the State, then I
submit that it must be shown that the State has taken
advantage of this provision of the Revised Statutes,
section 134, or the single vote is lost.

The question came directly before the judges of the
Supreme Court of Rhode Island, in the case of George

H. Corliss, who held the office of member of the Centennial Commission under the United States on the day of the presidential election. The governor, under the authority of the statutes, submitted to the judges of the Supreme Court of that State five questions : First, whether the office of centennial commissioner was an office of trust and profit, which they answered, by a majority of voices, it was, such as disqualified the holder for the office of elector of President and Vice-President. Secondly, whether the candidate who received a plurality of votes created a vacancy by declining the office. Thirdly, whether the disqualification was removed by the resignation of the said office of trust or profit. Fourthly, whether the disqualification resulted in the election of the candidate next highest in number of votes, or in failure to elect. Fifthly, if by reason of the disqualification of the candidate who received the plurality of the votes given there was no election, could the General Assembly in grand committee elect an elector ?

The judges answered the first question, as I said, by a majority of voices, that it was a disqualifying fact, this office of Commissioner of the United States Centennial Commission, and, by all their voices agreeing, answered that "such candidate who received a plurality declining the office did not create a vacancy ;" that the disqualification was not removed by the resignation of the office, but that the disqualification did not result in the election of the candidate next in vote, but did result in a failure to elect, and that there was no election, so that the General Assembly in grand committee might elect, and the General Assembly in grand committee did elect.

The opinion is signed by all the judges, Thomas Durfee, W. S. Burges, E. R. Potter, Charles Matteson,

and Stiness. It was a question submitted under the
constitution and laws of that State. I read it at this time
in order that I may if possible satisfy the Commission
that the construction which I place on section 134 of
the revised statutes is the correct construction.

In answer to the fourth question, which was this, "If
not, does the disqualification result in the election of
the candidate next in vote or in a failure to elect," the
court answered :

We think the disqualification does not result in the election of
the candidate next in vote, but in a failure to elect.

In England it has been held that where electors vote for an ineligible candidate, knowing his disqualification, their votes are
not to be counted, any more than if they were thrown for a dead
man or the man in the moon, and that in such a case the opposing
candidate, being qualified, will be elected, although he has had a
minority of the votes.

And such is the rule in Indiana and as was established
at an early day in Maryland by Chief Justice Samuel
Chase, of that State, and has continued in force, as I
am informed, down to this time, and been enforced
very recently. The judges of Rhode Island sustain this by the following references : King v. Hawkins,
10 East. 210 ; Reg. v. Coaks, 3 El. & B. 253.

But even in England, if the disqualification is unknown, the
minority candidate is not entitled to the office, the election being
a failure. (Queen v. Hiornes, 7 Ad. & E. 960; Rex v. Bridge,
1 M. & Selw. 76.) And it has been held that to entitle the minority candidate to the office it is not enough that the electors
knew of the facts which amount to a disqualification, unless they
likewise knew that they amount to it in point of law. (The
Queen v. The Mayor, etc., Law Rep., 3 Q. B. 629.)

In this country the law is certainly not more favorable to the minority candidate. (State v. Giles, 1 Chandler (Wis.) 112 ; State
v. Smith, 14 Wis. 497; Saunders v. Haynes, 13 Cal. 145 ; People v. Clute, 50 N. Y. 451.) The question submitted to us does
not allege or imply that the electors, knowing the disqualification,

voted for the ineligible candidate in willful defiance of the law; and certainly, in the absence of proof, it is not to be presumed that they so voted. The only effect of the disqualification, in our opinion, is to render void the election of the candidate who is disqualified, and to leave one place in the electoral college unfilled.

The answer to the fifth question, " If by reason of the disqualification of the candidate who received a plurality of the votes given there was no election, can the General Assembly in grand committee select an elector," was in the affirmative. The court, in discussing another question, had cited the seventh section of the General Statutes of Rhode Island, chapter 11, to wit:

If any electors, chosen as aforesaid, shall, after said election, decline the said office, or be prevented by any cause from serving therein, the other electors, when met in Bristol in pursuance of this chapter, shall fill such vacancies.

They had decided that disqualification did not create a case of vacancy. They then considered another statute of Rhode Island, which they held to have been passed under the authority confided to the State of Rhode Island by the one hundred and thirty-fourth section of the Revised Statutes:

" Our statute (General Statute, ch. 11, sec. 5) provides that if, by reason of the votes being equally divided, or otherwise, there shall not be an election of the number of electors to which the State may be entitled, the governor shall forthwith convene the General Assembly at Providence for the choice of electors to fill such vacancy by an election in grand committee." We think this provision covers the contingency which has happened, and that, therefore, the General Assembly in grand committee can elect an elector to fill up the number to which the State is entitled. The law of the United States provides that " whenever any State has held an election for the purpose of choosing electors, and has failed to make choice on the day prescribed by law, the electors may be appointed on a subsequent day, in such manner as the Legislature of the State may direct."

We have, then, the unanimous opinion of all the judges
of Rhode Island to the effect that the distinction on
which we insist is well taken, that the acts of Congress
are furnished for the purpose of covering all the cases
that may arise, in order that the constitutional provision may have full force and effect; and yet that the State
may not be deprived of its opportunity to be fully rep-
resented in the electoral college. The inhibition of the
constitution being peremptory, and like all the inhibi-
tions, whether express or implied, self-enforcing, were
there no such provision as that contained in section
134, the vote of the State would necessarily be lost,
unless it could be shown by some principle of law, by
the authority of some decided case, that the election of
a disqualified candidate is possible notwithstanding the
disqualification contained in a constitutional inhibition
of the character here referred to.

But peradventure by mistake, and without the intent
to violate the spirit of the constitutional provision, by
mere misadventure the State may have selected as one
of its electors or as all of its electors persons holding
disqualified offices, and, therefore, said Congress, whenever there be a case of non-election in any State the Legislature may provide a method of supplying the defect, and whenever there be a case of vacancy the Legislature may provide a method of supplying the defect;
a vacancy which occurs when the college of elected electors meets, a non-election which occurs when an election
has been held. If no election has been held, there is no
provision of statutory law to meet the case at all; but
the one hundred and thirty-third section provides for
the case of a vacancy when there has been a qualified
person elected, and the one hundred and thirty-fourth
section provides for the case of non-election when an
election has been held. It does not contemplate the

case where no election at all has been held, but it explicitly provides for a case where an election has been held which has not resulted in the choice of a competent and qualified candidate, and furnished to the people of the State of Florida, as it did to the State of Rhode Island, ample opportunity to save themselves from all misadventure, from all the consequences of mistake, or ignorance, or innocent evil, by enabling them to have a second opportunity, notwithstanding the constitutional provision that Congress may determine the time of choosing the electors.

ELECTORAL VOTE OF THE STATE OF OREGON.

On Wednesday, February 21, 1877, *the Electoral Commission held an evening session in the Senate Chamber, when Mr.* HOADLY *delivered the following argument on behalf of the electoral votes cast, in the State of Oregon, by* E. A. CRONIN, J. N. T. MILLER, *and* JOHN PARKER, *and contained in certificate No.* 2, *and against the electoral votes contained in certificate No.* 1, *opened by the President of the Senate, containing the votes of* JOHN W. WATTS, WILLIAM H. ODELL, *and* JOHN C. CARTWRIGHT, *for Hayes and Wheeler.*

MR. PRESIDENT AND GENTLEMEN OF THE COMMISSION : The first proposition to which I address myself is that the decisions made by the Commission in the cases of Florida and Louisiana, applied to this case, require the Commission to sustain the electoral votes cast by Cronin, Miller, and Parker, namely, one for Tilden and Hendricks, and two for Hayes and Wheeler. Without retracing its steps and withdrawing the conclusions the Commission has announced in the cases of Florida and Louisiana, the result can not be reached which is desired by our learned antagonists.

In order that we may in the briefest possible manner ascertain the point of contention, I will read from the decision of this Commission in the case of Louisiana :

And the Commission has by a majority of votes decided and does hereby decide that it is not competent under the Constitution and the law as it existed at the date of the passage of said act to go into evidence *aliunde* the papers opened by the President of the Senate in the presence of the two Houses to prove that other persons than those regularly certified to by the governor of the State of Louisiana, on and according to the determination and declaration of their appointment by the returning officers for election in the said State prior to the time required for the performance of their duties, had been appointed electors, or by counter-proof to show that they had not; or that the determination of the said returning officers was not in accordance with the truth and the fact; the Commission by a majority of votes being of opinion that it is not within the jurisdiction of the two Houses of Congress assembled to count the votes for President and Vice-President to enter upon a trial of such questions.

I do not understand that this is a ruling upon a mere question of proof, but that it is a ruling upon a high proposition of jurisdiction. Nor do I understand that by this decision is meant that anything and everything which any person claiming to be an elector may enclose in an envelope and address to the President of the Senate has the force of testimony before this honorable Commission, but only that those documents and papers which if offered *aliunde* would be competent, may be considered when found within the envelopes, and that the determination and decision of the returning board of a State, acted upon by the governor of the State in the manner provided in the one hundred and thirty-sixth section of the Revised Statutes, is final and conclusive, and that the names therein contained are the names of the true and valid electors of the State.

That I am right in this construction of this decision is confirmed by the views of one for whom long knowledge has impressed me with great respect. I am not personally intimate with him, but intimate in the sense in which any citizen may be said to be intimate with the judgment, the opinions, and the habits of accuracy of statement of a statesman. I say, that I am right in this conclusion is confirmed by a statement of reasons for this conclusion given in the Senate of the United States on the 20th of February by a member of this Commission, the honored Senator from Indiana [Mr. MORTON]. He said:

The Constitution says the certificates shall be opened by the President of the Senate in the presence of the two Houses. Whether he is to count the votes or whether the two Houses are to count the votes, and I assume under this law the two Houses are to do it, or in certain cases this Electoral Commission, what can they do? They have but one duty to perform, and that is to ascertain that these certificates came from the electors of the State. When that is done " the vote shall then be counted." They must ascertain the fact whether they came from the electors of the State; and when they have ascertained that their duty is at an end. There is no time, there is no place to try any question of ineligibility or of election when the votes are to be counted. And how are we to know that the certificates came from the electors of the State? In the first place the act of Congress provides *prima facie* evidence, the governor's certificate, but that is not conclusive. That is the result of an act of Congress. Congress may repeal that act or it may provide by another to go behind it, but when you go behind that and come to the action of the officers of the State, there your inquiry is at an end. Whenever the officers appointed by a State to declare who have been chosen electors have acted and made that declaration, it is final so far as Congress is concerned. The action of the State officers is the act of the State.

With this statement of principle I am content. My proposition is that the State of Oregon, through her State officers, through her governor, supported by her canvassing board, has spoken, and the result of her speech is here in the certificates of E. A. Cronin, William H. Odell, and John C. Cartwright, which certificates are attached to the votes of Cronin, Miller, and Parker, and are the only legitimate, lawful evidence of the act of Oregon, without which the pretended votes of Odell, Cartwright, and Watts fail to have any legal effect whatever.

The views expressed by Senator Morton find confirmation in the case of Dennett, petitioner, in volume 32 of the Reports of the State of Maine, page 508. The opinion was pronounced by Shepley, chief-justice, and there was no dissenting opinion:

The act of opening and comparing the votes returned for county commissioners can not be performed by the persons holding the offices of governor and of councilors, unless they act in their official capacities, for it is only in that capacity that the power is conferred upon them. The duty is to be performed upon the responsibility of their official stations and under the sanctity of their official oaths. The governor and council, and not certain persons that may be ascertained to hold those offices, must determine the number of votes returned for each person as county commissioner, and ascertain that some one has or has not a sufficient number to elect him.

It is, then, the State of Oregon which speaks when the governor, under section 136 of the Revised Statutes of the United States, in obedience to the return and canvass of the returning officers, to the declaration and determination of the result of the canvass by the returning officers, issues that certificate.

It shall be the duty of the executive of each State—

Says the statute—

to cause three lists of the names of the electors of such State to be made and certified, and to be delivered to the electors on or before the day on which they are required by the preceding section to meet.

Again, section 138:

The electors shall make and sign three certificates of all the votes given by them, each of which certificates shall contain two distinct lists, etc.

And so the next section, that the certificates shall be sealed and delivered, one to the Federal district judge, one sent by mail to the President of the Senate, and one sent by messenger to the President of the Senate.

Now, I ask your honors' attention to the question, Who were the electors ascertained to be appointed by the official decision and determination (that I believe to have been the language used in the Florida case) of the board of State canvassers of the State of Oregon? Or, to use the language adopted in the Louisiana case, Who were the returning officers upon and according to whose determination of their appointment the governor acted or failed to act, as the case may be, in the issue of the certificates of the State of Oregon?

This leads us to an examination and comparison of the statutes of the State of Oregon in connection with the statutes of the States of Florida and Louisiana, for I refer to Florida and Louisiana, in order that we who are of counsel may have a guide to the real effect of the opinions already pronounced by this Commission. I mean of course in applying to the case of Oregon the decisions made by this Commission in the matter of Florida and Louisiana.

In Florida certain persons are to

form a board of State canvassers, and proceed to canvass the returns of said election, and determine and declare who shall have been elected to any such office or as such member, as shown by such returns.

Here the office of determination and declaration is superadded to the office of canvassing; and by a later provision in the same section the board are required to

make and sign a certificate containing in words written at full length the whole number of votes, etc.

And—

When any person shall be elected to the office of elector . . . the governor shall make out, sign, and cause to be sealed with the seal of the State, and transmit to such person a certificate of his election.

The point to which I desire particularly your attention is that, under the laws of Florida, the determination and decision are separated in legal thought, and thus, in legal act, from the canvass itself; and so we find it in Louisiana, as is made manifest in the oath that—

I will carefully and honestly canvass and compile the statements of the votes.

Again—

Within ten days after the closing of the election said returning officers shall meet in New Orleans to canvass and compile the statements of votes made by the commissioners of election, and make returns of the election to the secretary of state. They shall continue in session until such returns have been compiled. The presiding officer shall, at such meeting, open in the presence of the said returning officers the statements of the commissioners of election, and the said returning officers shall, from said statements, canvass and compile the returns of the election in duplicate ; one copy of such returns they shall file in the office of the secretary of state, and of one copy they shall make public proclamation, by printing in the official journal and such other newspapers as they may deem proper, declaring the names of all persons and officers voted for, the number of votes for each person, and the names of the persons who have been duly and lawfully elected. The returns of the election thus made and promulgated shall be *prima facie* evidence in all courts of justice and before all civil officers, until set aside after contest according to law, of the right of any person named therein to hold and exercise the office to which he shall by such return be declared elected. The governor shall, within thirty days thereafter, issue commissions to all officers thus declared elected, who are required by law to be commissioned.

Now in Oregon the language of the sixtieth section is this :

The votes for the electors shall be given, received, returned, and canvassed as the same are given, returned, and canvassed for members of Congress. The secretary of state shall prepare two lists of the names of the electors elected, and affix the seal of the State to the same, etc.

I will come back to that presently. Let us now see how votes are given, received, returned, and canvassed for members of Congress. Section 37 is:

The county clerk, immediately after making the abstract of the votes given in his county, shall make a copy of each of said abstracts, and transmit it by mail to the secretary of state, at the seat of government; and it shall be the duty of the secretary of state, in the presence of the governor, to proceed, within thirty days after the election, and sooner if the returns be all received, to canvass the votes given for secretary and treasurer of state, state printer, justices of the supreme court, members of Congress, and district attorneys.

If this were all the statute, an argument by implication might be made, to the effect that the duty to canvass involves the duty to determine the results of the canvass. But this is not all, for the governor, who is required to be present, is not an idle spectator, as is claimed by the objectors to certificate No. 2:

And the governor shall grant a certificate of election to the person having the highest number of votes, and shall also issue a proclamation declaring the election of such person.

And this is made perfectly plain by the next sentence:

In case there shall be no choice by reason of any two or more persons having an equal and the highest number of votes for either of such offices, the governor shall, by proclamation, order a new election to fill said offices.

For what purpose is the governor present? He is to witness the canvass and declare its result, and his declaration of its result is the certificate he gives, and his proclamation declaring the election of such person. He is not there by way of idle ceremony any more than the two Houses of Congress are present at the opening of the envelopes as a mere idle ceremony. He is there to do what is required of him to do—to witness the canvass and to declare its result. But if this be not so in the matter of members of Congress of Oregon, it is unquestionably so with regard to the final determination, decision, and declaration of the result of the election of electors. The secretary of state is to canvass. No duty is imposed on him to declare any result whatever. He is to canvass, and what is that canvass? I copied—perhaps it was an idle thing—from the approved lexicographers the definition of the word. Worcester says:

1. To sift; to examine; to scrutinize.
I have made careful search, and *canvassed* the matter with all possible diligence.— *Woodward.*
2. To debate; to discuss; to agitate.
They *canvassed* the matter one way and t'other.—*L'Estrange.*
To solicit votes from; to bespeak.

And Webster traces the origin of the word to the old French word *canebasser*, and defines it thus :

To examine curiously; to search or sift out, as canvass in Old English, and probably in Old French signified also a sieve, a straining-cloth.
1. To sift; to strain; to examine thoroughly; to search or scrutinize; as, to *canvass* the votes for senators.
2. To take up for discussion; to debate.
An opinion that we are likely soon to *canvass.*—*Sir W. Hamilton.*
3. To go through in the way of solicitation; as, to *canvass* a district for votes.

Here is no necessary implication that the word means "to determine the result." It is to examine, scrutinize, tabulate, and formulate, but not necessarily to ascertain and determine results, and so the word is used in Florida, and so the word is used in Louisiana, and so the corresponding word "examine," as I shall presently show you, is used in Massachusetts, and so the word is used in Oregon. When we come to the sixtieth section of the statute, we find that this view is confirmed. Let us now return to the sixtieth section :

The votes for the electors shall be given, received, returned and canvassed as the same are given, returned, and canvassed for members of Congress.

It does not say "given, received, returned, canvassed, and declared," or "given, received, returned, canvassed, and certified." It says, "given, received, returned, and canvassed," and the provision with regard to the final determination and decision is contained in the next clause of the section :

The secretary of state shall prepare two lists of the names of the electors *elected*, and affix the seal of the State to the same.

Two lists, not three ; the secretary of state, not the governor. It is not under the act of Congress that this is required, for the act of Congress calls for no great seal of Oregon, and calls for no certificate of the secretary of state of Oregon. The act of Congress calls for a certificate which may be without a seal, which may be without the attestation of a secretary. The act of Congress simply provides that it shall be the duty of the executive of each State to cause three lists of the names of the electors of such State to be made and certified.

But Oregon says:

The secretary of state shall prepare two lists of the names of the electors *elected*, and affix the seal of the State to the same. Such lists shall be signed by the governor and secretary, and by the latter delivered to the college of electors at the hour of their meeting on such first Wednesday of December.

And here are the lists prepared under this section, to which are signed the names of the governor and secretary, under the great seal of the State, declaring that William H. Odell, John C. Cartwright, and E. A. Cronin are the electors elected:

I, L. F. Grover, governor of the State of Oregon, do hereby certify that at a general election held in said State on the 7th day of November, A. D., 1876 William H. Odell received 15,206 votes, John C. Cartwright 15,214 votes, E. A. Cronin received 14,157 votes, for electors of President and Vice-President of the United States; being the highest number of votes cast at said election for persons eligible, under the Constitution of the United States, to be appointed electors of President and Vice-President of the United States, they are hereby declared duly elected electors as aforesaid for the State of Oregon.

This is the voice of Oregon, according to the judgment of this Commission in the cases of Florida and Louisiana. Its truthfulness has been impeached; but one thing I am certain I may say in this presence, it is as true as the certificates which have received the approval of this Commission coming from Florida and Louisiana.

They are duly elected. They are hereby declared—

duly elected electors as aforesaid for the State of Oregon.

LAFAYETTE GROVER,
Governor of Oregon.

Attest:

S. F. CHADWICK,
Secretary of State of Oregon.

But, says my learned friend, the secretary of state has simply signed it as a witness. Not so. He signed it in attestation of the truth of the fact. He is a participant in the declaration thereby He has attached the great sealh of the State. It is the act of the governor and the act of the secretary in the ordinary form, and being such, it is in compliance with the sixtieth

section of the statute of Oregon, and at the same time
with the one hundred and thirty-sixth section of the Revised Statutes of the United States, and thus constitutes
the final and conclusive decision and determination of
the vote of the State of Oregon, according to the only
evidence provided by law by which this tribunal can communicate with the State of Oregon. The laws of the
United States have provided but a single method by
which this tribunal can communicate with Oregon. It
is in the one hundred and thirty-sixth section of the Revised Statutes of the United States. There is the
method pointed out by law by which the voice of Oregon
may speak to this tribunal, to the two Houses of Congress, and which this tribunal, standing in the place of
the two Houses of Congress, may hear as the voice of
Oregon, as has been decided in the cases of Florida and
Louisiana.

I submit this proposition in connection, however,
with a decision in the State of Massachusetts.

Mr. Commissioner THURMAN. Who, by the laws
of Oregon, had the custody of the great seal of the
State?

Mr. HOADLY. I am unable to answer the question.

Mr. MATTHEWS. The secretary of state, by the Constitution.

Mr. HOADLY. It has been answered probably correctly. I do not mean by " probably correctly " to
impeach my learned friend. I meant——

Mr. MATTHEWS. The Constitution says so.

Mr. HOADLY. I have not looked at it; but I
say there is nothing in the laws of Oregon which requires any such certificate or exemplification as is presented by the supporters of certificate No. 1. It can
not be found there. There is the provision of Oregon,

section sixty, and the abstract, which is simply a certified statement of the number of votes received at the election, is a provision *aliunde* the laws of Oregon, although it was within the envelope opened by the President of the Senate.

Mr. Representative LAWRENCE. The secretary of state can certify at common law.

Mr. HOADLY. But the laws of Oregon have determined and prescribed who shall certify to this tribunal. That certificate we present.

Now I call your honors' attention to the opinion of the judges of the supreme judicial court of Massachusetts, signed by them all—Horace Gray, John Wells, James D. Colt, Seth Ames, Marcus Morton, William C. Endicott, and Charles Devens, jr., Boston, March 5, 1875—to be found on page 600 of the one hundred and seventeenth volume of Massachusetts Reports :

The seventh chapter of the general statutes has constituted the governor and council a board to *examine*, as soon as may be after receiving them, the returns of votes from the various cities and towns for district attorneys and other officers named in this article of the Constitution, and requires the governor forthwith to transmit to such persons as appear to be chosen to such offices a certificate of such choice, signed by the governor and countersigned by the secretary of the Commonwealth.

Notice, the governor and council are obliged to examine the returns; it does not say "to examine and declare the result," but "to examine :"

The nature of the duties thus imposed and the very terms of the statute show that they are to be performed without unnecessary delay, and that the certificate issued by the governor to any person appearing upon such examination to be elected is the final and conclusive evidence of the determination of the governor and council as to his election.

I submit that by parity of reasoning the certificate or

list signed by the governor and secretary of state of
Oregon, under the great seal of the State, and by the
latter delivered to the college of electors at the hour of
their meeting on the first Wednesday of December, is
the final and conclusive evidence of the determination
of the governor and secretary as to their election. Why
are the governor and secretary required to sign these
lists ? It is that the chief executive of the State and
the canvassing officer shall unite in declaring who are
elected. The secretary, the canvassing officer, is required to prepare two lists of the names of electors
elected, and to affix the great seal of the State to the
same ; and the governor, in whose presence the canvass
is made, must also sign, and together their signatures,
with the great seal of the State, constitute the final and
conclusive, irrefragible evidence who are the electors of
the State of Oregon.

I pass from this proposition to consider another. It
is a familiar proposition of law that when a commission
or certificate of election has been delivered to an officer,
and he accepts it, and enters upon the performance of
the duties of that office, he becomes an officer *de jure et
de facto*, and is to be so treated in all courts, in all places,
under all circumstances, except when his title may be impeached by *quo warranto, certiorari*, or proceeding under
a statute for contest. This evidence is here presented by
E. A. Cronin, J. N. T. Miller, and John Parker. They
come here, Cronin, as a certificated elector, having
vouched in Miller and Parker to vote with him in consequence of the refusal of Cartwright and Odell to act
with him. I will stop a moment simply to say that in
my judgment the statements contained in the record in
connection with certificate No. 2 are confirmed and
placed beyond the possibility of a doubt by the statements contained in certificate No. 1. Mr. Cronin says

(and he presents the authentic, official advice to this Commission of his election and the election of Odell and Cartwright) that they refused to act with him, and they say that they were elected with Watts, and that they organized with Watts by accepting the resignation of Watts and electing into the place, thus made vacant by the declination of Watts, Mr. Watts himself.

I respectfully submit, Mr. President and gentlemen of the Commission, that there is no contradiction between these certificates. Mr. Cronin was in possession of the official decision and determination of the canvassers of Oregon. He proposed to act. Mr. Watts' name is not in the official decision and determination of the canvassers of Oregon, but was excluded by them. Mr. Watts proceeded to act with Odell and Cartwright. They did not say, as my learned friend who closed the argument for the objectors would have this Commission to understand, that they (Odell and Cartwright with Cronin) made the board, and that Cronin refused to act with them. There can be no refusal without an opportunity. They proceeded to exclude Cronin by accepting Watts' resignation.

Mr. Commissioner ABBOTT. Is there any allegation anywhere on that certificate that they refused to act with Cronin or Cronin refused to act with them?

Mr. HOADLY. Cronin's name is not in that certificate. He is ignored utterly and entirely. Odell and Cartwright state that they acted with Watts, that they accepted Watt's resignation, and elected Watts to take the place of Watts, all the while it being shown by the official decision and determination that Cronin was ready to act, Cronin alleging, with Miller and Parker, that they refused to act with him, and they alleging, without naming him, that they refused to act with him by alleging that they did act without him and with Watts.

I was wrong in saying that their record does not name Cronin. It does name him, but it names him to confirm the statement I have just made. Certificate No. 1 says that Odell and Cartwright required of the governor and the secretary of state certified lists, which both those officers refused to give them, thus adding to their official decision and determination a refusal to give such evidence to anybody else.

And so far as evidence *aliunde* the lists may be considered (a question which this Commission may yet be called upon to decide) they do say :

And being informed that such lists had been delivered to one E. A. Cronin, by said secretary state, we, each and all—

That is, Watts, Odell, and Cartwright, each and all—

demanded such certified lists of said E. A. Cronin ; but he then and there refused to deliver or to exhibit such certified lists to us or either of us.

And, therefore, Mr. Cronin produces the lists which do not contain the name of Watts.

I was going on to say that a certificated or commissioned officer who enters upon the discharge of duty is an officer *de jure et de facto* in all tribunals, in all places, with reference to any action of his in his office, until challenged by writ of *quo warranto*, or contest of election, or writ of *certiorari*. The lists provided for by the one hundred and thirty-sixth section of the Revised Statutes and the sixtieth section of the statutes of Oregon being held by E. A. Cronin did make him an elector *de jure et de facto* as to all persons, except the State challenging upon *quo warranto*, or except upon *certiorari*, or except upon contest of election ; and to that proposition I desire to direct a few remarks, which will be mainly by way of referring to authority.

I will read first from the case of the People *v.* Miller, 16 Michigan Reports, page 56. It is the opinion of his honor, Mr. Justice Christiancy, concurred in by Judge Cooley and Judge Campbell, and I am sure I need not say in this hall that an opinion from such a source, with such confirmation, can not be challenged with safety in any court of justice in the land.

The certificate of election, whether rightfully or wrongfully given, confers upon the person holding it the *prima facie* right of holding it for the term, and this *prima facie* right is subject to be defeated only by his voluntary surrender of the office, or by a judicial determination of the right. We do not mean to say that if the respondent had abandoned or should abandon his claim to the office under the election, witnessed by the certificate admitting the relator's right, that the board might not have received and approved the relator's bond, but they certainly had no jurisdiction to try the validity of the election as between the relator and the respondent, and in such a contest the certificate of election was conclusive upon them until the right should be judicially tried

The head-note or syllabus of the case is :

The certificate of election, whether rightfully or wrongfully given by the board of canvassers, confers upon the person holding it the *prima facie* right to the office until his right is rejected by a voluntary surrender or by a judicial determination against him.

This proposition has been three times decided in the State of Pennsylvania, in cases to which I will direct your honors, beginning with the case of Commonwealth *ex relatione* Ross *v.* Baxter, 35 Pennsylvania State Reports, p. 263 :

A return by the election officers that A B received a majority of the votes for a township office is legal and *prima facie* evidence of his title to the office ; and it can only be set aside by proceedings for a false return under the act of July 2, 1839. It can not be inquired into by *quo warranto.*

So in the forty-first volume Pennsylvania State Reports, Hulseman and Brinkworth *v.* Rems and Siner, page 401, a case of great interest in many respects. I read from pages 400 and 401. It was an action in equity for an injunction, for in Pennsylvania it is held that a conflict between two officers claiming in conflicting rights may be decided under certain circumstances by injunction in equity.

We have, therefore, no ground left for our interference but the single one that the return judges included in their enumeration returns purporting to be from three companies of volunteers, which were forgeries. We admit, therefore, that the evidence proves that these certificates of the election of the defendants are founded in manifest fraud, the forgery of some unknown person, but we do not find that the defendants had any hand in it; and we trust they had not. Can we on this account interfere and declare the certificates void?

Mr. Commissioner HOAR. Who were the defendants in that case?

Mr. HOADLY. It was a proceeding in equity by John Hulseman and George Brinkworth, citizens and qualified voters, against James Rems and Charles B. Siner.

Mr. Commissioner HOAR. Were they the persons claiming the office?

Mr. HOADLY. They were the persons claiming the office and holding the certificates of election.

According to our laws the election has passed completely through all its forms, the result has been in due form declared and certified, and the defendants have received their certificates of election, and are entitled to their seats as members of the common council. The title-papers of their offices are complete, and have the signatures of the proper officers of the law; and if they are vitiated by any mistake or fraud in the process that has produced them, this raises a case to be tried by the forms of " a contested election " before the tribunal appointed by law to try such questions, and not by the ordinary forms of legal or equitable process before the usual judicial tribunals.

In Kerr and others ·v. Trego and others, 47 Pennsylvania State Reports, page 292, the syllabus is:

> In all bodies that are under law, where there has been an authorized election for the office in controversy, the certificate of election which is sanctioned by law or usage is the *prima facie* written title to the office, and can only be set aside by a contest in the forms prescribed by law.

To the same effect the case of the People *v.* Cook, in 4 Selden's Reports, page 68 :

> The certificate of the board of canvassers may be conclusive of the election of an officer in a controversy arising collaterally, or between the party holding it and a stranger. But between the people and the party in an action to impeach it, it is only *prima facie* evidence of the right. It is the will of the electors and not the certificate which gives the right to the office.

So again in 33 New York reports. I will read from page 606, the case of Hadley *v.* Mayor. It was a case of a policeman suing for salary. In other words, it was an action in which the question arose, as it arises here, collaterally ; it did not arise by *quo warranto ;* it did not arise by *certiorari ;* it did not arise by contest ; it arose as here :

> The second exception was to the decision by which the court excluded the inspector's returns. The object, I suppose, was to show that the returns elected Mr. Quackenbush and not Mr. Perry. But the law having committed to the common council the duty of canvassing the returns and determining the result of the election from them, and the council having performed that duty and made a determination, the question as to the effect of the returns was not open for a determination by a jury in an action in which the title of the officer came up collaterally. If the question had arisen upon an action in the nature of a *quo warranto* information, the evidence would have been competent. But it would be in-

tolerable to allow a party affected by the acts of a person claiming to be an officer to go behind the official determination to prove that such official determination arose out of mistake or fraud.

So also in Dutcher's Reports, New Jersey, page 355, the case of the State *v.* The Clerk of the County of Passaic:

A *quo warranto* is the legal and usual mode in which title to office may be tried and finally adjudicated.

The determination of the board of county canvassers has no such final effect as to interfere with a full investigation of the result of an election upon a writ of *quo warranto.*

Again, on page 356:

In the present instance, the writ appears to have been designed as ancillary to the application for a mandamus, in order to bring before the court the decision of the board of county canvassers and the evidence upon which it was founded. That application having been denied, and the office having been filled, a decision upon the validity of the proceedings of the board would be nugatory. It would neither vacate the commission which has been issued nor avail the plaintiff in any subsequent proceedings which may be instituted to determine his rights. If the determination of the board of county canvassers partakes at all of the character of a judicial act, it certainly has no such final or conclusive effect as to interfere with the full and free investigation of the legal result of the election upon a writ of *quo warranto.*

So in Minnesota, in the fifteenth volume of Minnesota Reports, page 455, the decision of a court, one of the judges of which is now a member of the United States Senate (Mr. McMillan), State of Minnesota *ex rel.* R. A. Briggs *v.* O. A. Churchill, auditor, etc:

Under the laws of this State the result of the canvass by a board of county canvassers is a decision and determination of the election of the persons whom they declare to be elected.

The abstract of the canvass of the votes in the form prescribed in the statute is the authentic and official evidence of the canvass by the board by which the county auditor is to be governed in issuing the certificates of election.

When a certificate of election is issued and delivered by the auditor to a person declared to be elected to a county office, in accordance with the official canvass, regular upon its face, the certificate is conclusive evidence of the right of the person holding it to the office to which it shows him to have been elected, *except* in a proceeding where this right is directly in issue. To go behind a certificate thus issued and determine the correctness of the canvass involves the determination of 'the right of the holder of the certificate to the office; this can not be done upon mandamus.

And so in three cases in the twenty-fifth volume of the Louisiana Reports. Certainly whatever authority this volume may have, whatever respect or want of respect may be shown to it, it is not for those who have sustained before this tribunal the acts of the State government of which the authors of this volume are part and parcel, to challenge the decision made by the court of which Mr. Ludeling was chief-justice. In The State *v.* Wharton, page 3, they say :

Where two sets of officers claim to be the legal board of returning officers, it is difficult to conceive why this is not a judicial question.

In Collin *v.* Knoblock and others, page 263, they say :

The adjustment and compilation of election returns, determining the number of legal and illegal votes cast for each candidate, declaring the result of an election and furnishing the successful candidate with the proper certificate, in short superintending and controlling all the details of an election, belong properly to the political department of the government.

In The State on the relation of Bonner *v.* Lynch, page 267, they say :

The defendant having been returned by the legal returning board of the State as elected judge of the fourth district court of

New Orleans, and upon that return the acting governor having issued a commission to him according to law, it can not be said that one holding an office under such a commission has intruded into or unlawfully holds the office.

In the twentieth volume of Vermont Reports, page 473, in the case of Overseer of the Poor of Norwich *v.* Halsey J. Yarrington, the court say:

When a person acting as justice of the peace holds a commission for that office from the governor, under the seal of the State, the court will not go behind that commission to inquire whether he had been duly appointed to that office by the General Assembly of the State or not.

So in three cases in the State of Ohio.

Mr. Commissioner MILLER. That was not in a proceeding directly against him to invalidate the act.

Mr. HOADLY. Of course if it had been a *quo warranto*, a *certiorari*, or a contest, the question would have arisen judicially and properly; but it was not. It was a complaint in bastardy, where the woman for the space of thirty days had neglected to charge the putative father, and a controversy thereupon arose.

So in three cases in the State of Ohio, in which it was decided by the supreme court of that State each time that a proceeding to try a title to an office was a judicial proceeding. In one of these cases the supreme judicial court of the State of Ohio were called upon to pass upon one of the most important questions that ever arose in the State. It had been held in the county of Wayne that John K. McBride was elected probate judge of the county of Wayne by reason of the decision that the law allowing the soldiers in the field, out of the State of Ohio, to vote, was not in conformity with the Constitution of the State of Ohio; and the cause was taken by writ of error to the supreme court of Ohio. The first question that court was called upon to decide was

whether this was a judicial question which could be
removed by petition in error, in accordance with our
forms of practice, to that court ; and the court decided
that it was—that a proceeding to contest the election
of John K. McBride was a judicial proceeding, and the
commission having been delivered to him, the decision
and ascertainment of who was the duly elected probate
judge of the county of Wayne was a judicial determination and decision in that cause. To the same
effect is the case of The State *v.* The Commissioners of Marion County (14 Ohio State Reports, 578),
and the case of Powers *v.* Reed and others (19 Ohio
State Reports, 205, 206), in which the question that
arose was whether the declaration of the result of
an election, upon which depended the change of the
county seat of Wood county from Bowling Green
to Perrysburgh, or from Perrysburgh to Bowling Green,
was a judicial determination, and it was argued before
the supreme court of Ohio, as your honors will find by
reference to that case, by one of the first lawyers in the
Western States, a gentleman who had filled the highest
places in the judicial department of the State of Ohio
—I mean Judge Ranney—and whose abilities are equal
to the positions he has held, that that question was a
political question and not a judicial question. But his
argument was overruled by the unanimous opinion of
the court.

So in the case of Morgan *v.* Quackenbush, which was
cited to us the other day—I will read a passage or two
—decided by Mr. Justice Ira Harris. I will read from
page 72 of 22 Barbour :

The certificate of a board of canvassers is evidence of the person upon whom the office has been conferred. Upon all questions
arising collaterally, or between a party holding a certificate and

a stranger, it is conclusive evidence; but in a proceeding to try the right to office, it is only *prima facie* evidence.

Again, on page 79:

If the certificate of the canvassers declaring Mr. Perry elected vested him with *colorable* title to the office, as I think it did, so that he had a right to enter upon the discharge of its duties, another effect of that decision was to exclude the defendant, Quackenbush, as well as everybody else, from the office. They could not hold as tenants in common, each having a legal right to perform its functions. If Mr. Perry became mayor *de facto*, the defendant Quackenbush, whatever his right, could not be mayor in fact at the same time.

My proposition is that E. A. Cronin became vested with the title and the office, if it may be called an office, at least with the right to discharge the trusts and functions of an elector, by the certificate of the governor of Oregon, attested by the secretary of state under the great seal of the State, and that this made him *de facto* elector, so that the office could not be held at the same time as tenant in common or otherwise by John W. Watts. He was the incumbent; and the only reply that I care to make to the argument which is founded on the statute of Oregon with regard to vacancies, is that the statute relates to and authorizes an incumbent to resign and does not authorize a claimant to resign, even though he be claiming *de jure* against an incumbent *de facto* holding. I am not now alluding to the statute of Oregon with regard to the election of electors, but to the statute in regard to filling vacancies in State offices. That I do not think your honors will find has any reference to this case at all under any circumstances.

Again, in Coolidge *v.* Brigham, 1 Allen, 335, Chief-Justice Bigelow, pronouncing the opinion of the whole court, said:

The magistrate before whom the action was originally brought was an officer *de facto*. He was not a mere usurper, undertaking to exercise the duties of an office to which he had no color of title. He had an apparent right to the office. He had a commission under the great seal of the State, bearing the signature of the governor, with his certificate thereon, that the oaths of office had been duly administered, and in all respects appearing to have been issued with the formalities required by the constitution and laws of the Commonwealth. He was thus invested with the apparent muniments of full title to the office. Although he might not have been an officer *de jure*, that is, legally appointed and entitled to hold and enjoy the office by a right which could not on due proceedings being had be impeached or invalidated, he was nevertheless in possession, under a commission *prima facie* regular and legal, and performing the functions of the office under a color and show of right. This made him a justice of the peace *de facto*.

So your honors will find, unless something can be discovered by more diligent search than I have made, and I have been very diligent, that when a man holds a certificate or a commission, whichever may be the ordinary evidence of title, and enters upon the possession of the office, he is an officer *de facto*, the office is full, there can be no other officer *de facto*. His title can only be impeached judicially. It may be taken from him by *quo warranto*; it may be taken by *certiorari*; it may be taken from him by proceedings to contest his election; but in the absence of these three methods of proceeding his title is perfect against all the world. Where is the *quo warranto* against E. A. Cronin? It may be said that there was a very short time in which to try it. No shorter, your honors, than was given in the case of Florida. Where is the *certiorari*? Where was the proceeding to contest? Here comes E. A. Cronin with the certificate of election under the great seal of Oregon, signed by the secretary of state, signed by the governor, and no judicial proceeding to impeach it. Is this tribunal a judicial tribunal? And were it a judicial tribunal, long ago the frauds that were offered to be proven to your honors in the case of Louisiana would have been heard and redressed. Were this a judicial tribunal, long ago the wrongs that were done in Florida would have been heard and redressed. But this is a legislative body, or part of a legislative body, delegates from the legislative body of the United States, without power to exercise any judicial function whatever. You can not try upon *quo warranto*; you can not try upon *certiorari*; you can not consider as upon proceedings to contest elections. The judicial power of the United States has been confided to the judges of the Supreme Court of the United States and of the inferior courts, and this is not the Supreme Court of the United States, nor any other court, inferior or otherwise.

If it be thought that my argument is inconsistent with what has been argued by others in the cases of Florida or Louisiana, I have to reply that it is consistent with perfect respect for the decisions of this tribunal. It is not for counsel to exhibit such disrespect to this tribunal as to attempt to overrule or overthrow its decisions. The object of this argument is to enforce the decisions of this tribunal and cause their application to the State of Oregon in such way that the decisions made in Florida and Louisiana shall not have the effect to reverse the judgment which the people of the United States on the 7th of November last pronounced. Your determination, which I have the right to cite as authority, written in your decisions, pronounced as the result of your conscientious examination, is here higher authority than any expression of persuasive opinion, however cogent, that I might quote from the decisions of courts, however respectable, and therefore I commend it to this tribunal as final and conclu-

sive evidence of the principles and rules of action which
this tribunal ought to adhere to and apply in this case.

But, if otherwise, I submit that, upon the merits of
this controversy, waiving for the present the propositions
I have made, your honors are required to decide in favor
of the Cronin vote. Here I desire to call your honors' attention to two propositions: First, that the papers inclosed with the certificate No. 1 are of no value
as evidence by being in that certificate or otherwise unless they are shown to be duly authenticated in conformity with the laws of Oregon. I read from section
78 of Freeman on Judgments:

> Nothing can be made a matter of record by calling it by that
> name, nor by inserting it among the proper matters of record.

And from 27 Connecticut Reports, Nichols *v.* City
of Bridgeport. This is not on my brief. The question was only called to my attention by hearing the debate of the objectors to certificate No. 2.

Mr. Commissioner GARFIELD. The point you are
making now is on your brief?

Mr. HOADLY. It is not. I did not know what was
contained in certificate No. 1 until this afternoon. I
read from 27 Connecticut, page 465:

> Between the reservation of the case and the term to which it
> had been continued to await our advice, it is obvious that there
> were no proceedings in the superior court, and that whatever
> proceedings took place in the case were in this court, and conse-
> quently that there were no proceedings, excepting the continu-
> ance of it, which it was the duty or province of the clerk of the
> superior court, or which it would have been proper for him to
> record as a part of the doings of that court; and, plainly, it is
> only of the doings of that court that the plaintiff in error can
> complain on this writ of error. Such being the case, the reserva-
> tion by that court can not properly be regarded as a part of its
> record, notwithstanding it has been inserted, as if it were a part
> of it, by the clerk, or certified by him to be such; for if it is not,

in its nature, a proper matter of record in the case, it can not be made such by the mere circumstance that it has been so inserted or attested. He can not make it a record, if, from its qualities, it is not so, either by treating it as such or calling it by that name.

And, secondly, a canvass is not even *prima facie* evidence of eligibility, as held by the Court of Appeals of Kentucky in Patterson *v.* Miller, etc., 2 Metc. Ky. 497 :

The certificate which the examining board issues to a candidate that he is elected to the office of sheriff—although conclusive evidence that he was elected thereto, unless his election be contested before the proper board—is not even *prima facie* evidence that he was eligible to the office.

In the next place the question arises, going behind these matters and going to what, if evidence were received, might be called the merits of the controversy— the question arises, What is the law of Oregon—not the general American public law, but the law of Oregon with regard to the election of electors under circumstances like the present? It has been argued and seriously claimed that the governor of Oregon had no right to pass upon the eligibility of electors ; that he was bound to see the Constitution of the United States violated ; that he was imbecile, without power. My friends seem to deal, as their stock in trade, in want of power, imbecility. It was the imbecility of this tribunal, according to their argument, which prevented the examination of the truth of the fact with regard to Florida and Louisiana, and now it is the imbecility of the governor of Oregon which will enable this tribunal to lend its aid to a violation of the Constitution of the United States, although the governor refused to be a partaker in that wrong. Let us see.

It is admitted that the law of Indiana is that where

there is an ineligible elector the governor not only may
but must take cognizance of the fact and refuse the
commission. It is admitted that this is the law of Indiana ; that the governor not only may but must recall
a commission once issued when the evidence of ineligibility growing out of a constitutional disqualification
is presented. If it be law in Indiana, why is it not law in
Oregon?' It is law in Arkansas ; it is law in Missouri ;
it is law in Rhode Island ; it is law in Massachusetts ;
it is law in Oregon ; and the authority for the statement
is the solemn adjudication of·the Supreme Court of each
one of these States ; in all but two, of the Court, judicially speaking, in a controversy between parties ; in
two, speaking in obedience to the constitution and
laws of the State in answer to a demand by the governor
for judicial information. It is the law of Arkansas ; so
held in two cases in the first volume of Arkansas reports (Pike's Reports), and one of those cases is that
which Senator Kelly began to read this afternoon, page
21, Taylor v. The Governor, which was a case where,
by the law of Arkansas, a defaulter in office was disqualified. There it was held by the Supreme Court of
that State that the governor had a right to take notice
of the disqualification and withhold the commission,
and not only that he had the right to do it, but that
it was his duty to do it. In the same volume, in a
later case, the exact proposition now under discussion
was at great length considered. I refer to the case of
Hawkins v. The Governor, pages 570 to 595. There
it is said :

Again, the executive is bound to see that the laws are faithfully executed ; and he has taken an oath of office to support
the constitution. How can he perform this duty if he has no
discretion left him in regard to granting commissions? For
should the Legislature appoint a person constitutionally ineligible

to hold any office of profit or trust, would the executive be bound
to commission him? and that, too, when his ineligibility was
clearly and positively proven? In such case the exercise of his
discretion must be admitted, or you make him, not the guardian,
but the violator of the constitution. What, then, becomes of his
oath of office?

Your honors, long, long ago, and by one of the greatest men who ever sat in judgment in the United States
of America, a man whose word is law to-day, though
the grass has been growing over his grave now for more
than half a century, the law was thus laid down :

It is argued—

Said Chief-Justice Parsons, in 5 Massachusetts, 533—

that the Legislature can not give a construction to the constitution,
can not make laws repugnant to it. But every department of
government invested with certain constitutional powers must, in
the first instance, but not exclusively, be the judge of its powers,
or it could not act.

In accordance with the same principle, in the great
case of Martin v. Mott, 12 Wheaton, 29, the President
of the United States was declared to be the final and
conclusive judge whether a case of insurrection existed
calling for the use of the military and naval forces of
the United States for its suppression. So it will be
found in the case of The State ex relatione Bartley v.
Fletcher, 39 Missouri, 388 ; and if your honors will
refer to the case of The State v. Vail, 53 Missouri, 97,
which was cited this afternoon by Mr. Lawrence, you
will find that the two cases can stand together. The
case of The State v. Vail does not overrule the Indiana
case of Gulick v. New, but cites it and distinguishes it.
But let me read a passage from 53 Missouri to show
that the case in Indiana is there cited and not dis-
approved :

But in the case in Indiana, it is conceded that where the candidate receiving the highest number of votes is ineligible by reason of a cause which the voters were not bound to know, such as non-age, want of naturalization, etc., the result is a failure to elect.

. . . .

It is unnecessary to determine whether it would be the rule, in any case of disqualifications, whether patent or latent.

Now come back to the case of the State on the relation of Bartley *v.* Fletcher, 39 Mo. 388. The opinion was pronounced by Mr. Justice Wagner. After reciting that it is by the constitution of the State made the duty of the governor to commission all officers not otherwise provided by law, that this is clearly an exercise of political power of a ministerial character, the court say :

The governor is bound to see that the laws are faithfully executed, and he has taken an oath to support the constitution. In the correct and legitimate performance of his duty he must inevitably have a discretion in regard to granting commissions ; for should a person be elected or appointed who was constitutionally ineligible to hold any office of profit or trust, would the executive be bound to commission him when his ineligibility was clearly and positively proven? If he is denied the exercise of any discretion in such case, he is made the violator of the Constitution, not its guardian. Of what avail then is his oath of office? Or if he has positive and satisfactory evidence that no election has been held in a county, shall he be required to violate the law and issue a commission to a person not elected, because a clerk has certified to the election? In granting a commission the governor may go behind the commission to determine whether an applicant is entitled to receive a commission or not where the objection to the right of the applicant to receive it rests upon the ground that a constitutional prohibition is interposed. Gulick *v.* New, 14 Ind. 93.

The issuing of a commission is an act by the executive in his political capacity, and is one of the means employed to enable him to execute the laws and carry on the appropriate functions of the State ; and for the manner in which he executes this duty he is in nowise amenable to the judiciary. The court can no

more interfere with executive discretion than the Legislature or
executive can with judicial discretion.

The granting of a commission by the executive is not a mere
ministerial duty, but an official act imposed by the constitution,
and is an investiture of authority in the person receiving it. We
are of the opinion, therefore, that mandamus will not lie against
the governor in a case like this.

So in the case in Maine, 7 Greenl. 497. In Maine
the language of the constitution is that a *majority* of
the votes shall elect, and yet to the opinion which was
read by Senator Kelly this afternoon declaring that by
that constitutional provision a majority of votes for
eligible candidates is meant are signed the honored names
of Prentiss Mellen and Nathan Weston, with their
associate, Albion K. Parris. Tell me that the opinion
that votes for ineligible candidates are void stands upon
no authority in America, when the name of one of the
greatest judicial lights that ever illumined the sky of
legal jurisprudence in New England and of another
second only to him are signed to that opinion !

This opinion comes first to us from one of the
signers of the Declaration of American Independence.
The first judgment ever pronounced in the United
States to the effect that a million of people voting for
an ineligible candidate can not defeat the mandate of the
Constitution to elect, came from Samuel Chase, who
long presided at the head of the judiciary of Maryland,
and as a member of the Supreme Court of the United
States, against whose temper much was said, but of
whose judicial judgments there has passed into history
no sound criticism whatever.

It has been said here this afternoon that a few insignificant opinions are to that effect. Yes, they are the
insignificant opinions of Samuel Chase, and Prentiss
Mellen, and Nathan Weston, and Albion K. Parris, and
Samuel E. Perkins, who, for a score of years has been
a judge of the Supreme Court of Indiana, and now by

the vote of the people last October has entered upon
another term of six years. The judicial opinions of
these men are those upon which this doctrine rests.
The time may come when justice, blind, deaf, and
robbed of the rest of her powers, may be wafted into
that Nirvana of intellectual inanition which the majority of the human race believe is reserved for that
which is absolutely perfect when its earthly work is done.
On that day the names of these great jurists and the
recollection of the wise counsels they have left us will
be forgotten among those who walk in the ways of
American jurisprudence according to the traditions of
the fathers, because on that day, but not sooner, a violation of the Constitution will become a muniment of
office.

But I was considering the question whether the governor had not furnished to us the final and conclusive
evidence of the law of Oregon, and I had cited the case
in Arkansas, the case in Missouri; I had not cited, but
I do now refer your honors to the opinion of Mr. Justice Cooley, as stated in his work on Constitutional
Limitations, page 41. I had cited the opinions of the
judges of Maine, in the seventh volume of Greenleaf's
Reports. I now ask your attention to the very recent
action of the judges and executive of the State of Rhode
Island, in the case of Corliss, which is precisely the
action which was taken in the case of Cronin by the
governor of Oregon. Had the governor of Oregon
been invested by the Constitution of Oregon with the
right to call for the opinions of the judges, and upon
that call received them, the action of Rhode Island and
the action of Oregon would have been precisely parallel.
In Rhode Island the governor was confronted by the fact
that George H. Corliss was a centennial commissioner
and that his name was on the roll of those receiving the

highest number of votes for electors. Did he give him
the certificate? Did he refuse the certificate? He refused. He called upon the judges of Rhode Island for
their judgment and advice. I have furnished the law
on this subject in my brief, and you will find, by reference to it, that the advice was given to him not as a
judicial judgment, but as advice for the guidance of his
executive action, and he acted. He called the Legislature together. He did not give the certificate to Corliss;
he withheld it from Corliss. He called the Legislature
together, and they elected Slater who received the certificate by force of the election by the Legislature.
So in Oregon; Senator Kelly read you this afternoon the
letter from the Chief-Justice of Oregon, from which it
appears that in the State of Oregon it has been judicially
determined that the governor has a right, although a
district attorney may be in office exercising the powers
and discharging the duties of the office, to declare the
office vacant, and where the Constitution has worked a
vacation of the office by reason of the incompatibility of
the two offices, to appoint a successor, and this action of
the governor in Oregon, in the case of Gibbs v. Bellin-
ger, was sustained by the supreme court of Oregon. The
opinion would have been pronounced and published in
the reports long ago but for the death of the lamented
Judge Thayer, by whom it was expected to be written.

So, I say that in Oregon as well as in Rhode Island,
in Maine, in Arkansas, in Missouri, we are fortified in
the opinion that the action of the governor in this case
was proper, and that it was and is the action of the executive, conclusive and final as evidence to this court of
what the law of Oregon is. Why, consider for one
moment. Suppose the governor had given a certificate
to Mr. Watts, notwithstanding his disqualification,
would not that have been evidence that Mr. Watts was

the elector ? Would it not have been cited as evidence that the law of Oregon was that, notwithstanding the disqualification, Mr. Watts had a right to the certificate ? Was not the governor called upon, compelled to elect which horn of the dilemma, if it were such, he would choose ; which view of the law at least he would take ? Could he avoid it ? He must say, by giving the certificate to Watts, " Notwithstanding the Constitution of the United States, and although the Constitution of Oregon says that I am to maintain the laws, notwithstanding this man is disqualified by law, he shall have the certificate." What is the Constitution of Oregon in this particular ? Let me read the passage. Section 10, article 5, of the executive department says, that " he " (the governor) " shall take care that the laws be faithfully executed." And he is sworn to support the Constitution of the United States and of Oregon ; yet it is said that he, bound to see that the laws were faithfully executed and to maintain the Constitution of the United States, violated his duty in not giving to one disqualified by the Constitution of the United States a certificate of election !

In the next place there was no vacancy into which Watts could be elected. First, there was an officer, if it may be called such, an elector holding office *de facto*, and I refer to the case read the other day by the learned senior counsel on the other side from the eleventh volume of Sergeant and Rawle. I refer to the passages which were read by him to show that when there is in office an officer *de facto* he completes the whole circumference of the office and occupies it all, and that there can be no vacancy and can be no intrusion upon him while he occupies, otherwise than by the action of a court of justice acting judicially.

Also, there was no vacancy, for the reason that by the

laws of the United States contemplation is made of two
contingencies, namely, a failure to elect, and a vacancy
when the electors meet ; and this was the first of these
two cases.   Upon this subject I have already been
heard in the Florida case by the Commission.

My learned friend, if he will allow me to call him
such (Mr. Evarts), informed us the other day that there
is no choice ; we have to say office filled or office vacant ;
there is no *tertium quid,* no *via media* in which our
footsteps may be safely directed.   But such is not
the law of the Senate of the United States as held in
this Chamber.   I say that the Senate of the United
States, from the foundation of the Government, has
never deviated from the rule that the office of Senator
can not be filled by the appointment of the governor
of a State when the Legislature has failed to elect an
incumbent during its session, as is shown by Lanman's
case.   Clark & Hall, 871.

But I am told that the House decided otherwise.
Aye, the House did decide, and if my friend (Mr.
Matthews) had not stopped with his reading of history just where he did, you would have learned all
that the House decided in the case to which he referred.   I do not consider the decision of a partisan
House in times of hot party politics as of much value,
and I certainly do not count the decision which was
reached by 118 yeas against 101 nays on the 3d day of
October, 1837, giving to Claiborne and Gholson their
seats as Representatives from the State of Mississippi,
as authority when I find that in the list of negative
votes are inscribed the names of John Quincy Adams
and Millard Fillmore, of John Sergeant and Richard
Fletcher, of John Bell and Thomas Corwin, of Caleb
Cushing and R. M. T. Hunter, of Henry A. Wise
and George Evans, of Elisha Whittlesey and James

Harlan and Thomas M. T. McKennan. That is a roll of names before which I bow as possessing greater authority than the whole list of the 1⊦8 who voted in the affirmative. But the record of the House does not stop there. On Monday, the 5th day of February, 1838 (page 160 of the sixth volume of the Congressional Globe,) on motion of John Bell, of Tennessee, by a vote of 121 yeas to 113 nays, the following resolution was adopted :

Resolved, That the resolution of this House of the 3d of October last declaring that Samuel J. Gholson and John F. H. Claiborne were duly elected members of the Twenty-fifth Congress be rescinded, and that Messrs. Gholson and Claiborne are not duly elected members of the Twenty-fifth Congress.

First, on adopting this as an amendment, the yeas were 119, the nays 112, and, secondly, on adopting the resolution as thus amended, the yeas were 121, the nays 113. And this is "the sober second thought" of the House of Representatives of 1837 and 1838 on this question.

Mr. Commissioner EDMUNDS. Is there not something peculiar in the conclusion respecting the filling of the office of a Senator by a governor growing out of the language of the Constitution, that where a vacancy shall happen during the recess of the Legislature the governor may fill it by a commission, which shall hold until the next meeting of the Legislature? Does not that have some bearing upon the subject?

Mr. HOADLY. No doubt. I do not claim that all the cases are *precisely* parallel.

Mr. Commissioner HOAR. What was the point decided in that case? Be good enough to state it.

Mr. HOADLY. The point was that neither Claiborne and Gholson nor Prentiss and Word were duly elected Representatives in the Twenty-fifth Congress.

Mr. Commissioner HOAR. That was not the point decided ; that was the fact.

Mr. HOADLY. The point decided was that the resolution adopted on the 3d of October, to which reference was made the other day, awarding to Claiborne and Gholson their seats as members of the Twenty-fifth Congress, should be *rescinded*.

Mr. Commissioner HOAR. My question was, what was the principle of law which was decided and for which you cited that case?

Mr. HOADLY. It is extremely difficult to answer that question. There may have been differences of opinion among those voting. I do not cite this case as authority, but it having been cited in authority against me the other day, I state the whole of the facts of the case in order that it shall not be vouched in any longer as authority upon the other side. Of course, there was a political controversy, and my own opinion is, if I may be allowed to state it, that the party feeling of the supporters of Mr. Van Buren and the antagonists of his administration had much more to do with the result than any judicial considerations whatever.

Mr. Commissioner HOAR. Was it not a case where an extra session was called and gentlemen from Mississippi were chosen before the general law permitted them to be chosen, on proclamation of the governor ?

Mr. HOADLY. That was the case.

Mr. MATTHEWS. Allow me to interrupt a moment. I would ask you whether or not the resolution of the House of Representatives admitting Claiborne and Gholson to the extra session was not that there was a vacancy in the representation of Mississippi in the House of Representatives in consequence of the expiration of the terms of the previous members of Con-

gress, and the fact that the election for the members of
the next Congress did not occur until the following November, and did not the Governor of Mississippi cause
that vacancy to be filled by a proclamation, in which he
called upon electors to elect Representatives to fill that
vacancy? Was not the resolution admitting them as
members of the Congress rescinded at the regular session because they were elected only to fill a vacancy?

Mr. HOADLY. I will answer by saying that the
whole statement is correct except the "because." It
was rescinded. Now, rescinding means withdrawing
the original proposition, and that is the language used.
It was not by virtue of a vote that, the vacancy having
expired or the time having expired, therefore they were
no longer members. But Mr. Bell's amendment was
that the original resolution should be rescinded.

This reminds me of another matter which I had al-
most forgotten, and that is that my friends may pos-
sibly cite against me the decision of the United States
House of Representatives in what is known as the
"broad-seal case" from New Jersey, a debate in which
the learned President of this Commission participated
as a member of the House. My answer to that, if it
be cited against me, will be that it was before a House
who were the judges of the returns and qualifications
of their own members; and a reference to Cooley, page
133, will show that this is a judicial power expressly
conferred upon the House.

This reminds me also of a case famous in the annals
of Ohio, and which ought to be famous in the annals
of the Federal Union, where a question once arose between the certificate of the returning officer and the abstract of the votes, in which the judgment arrived at
was most conspicuous and most beneficent. In the year
1848 the clerk of the court of common pleas of the

county in which I live, who, by law, was the returning officer, certified under the seal of the county that George E. Pugh, Alexander Long, and their associates were elected representatives to the Legislature of Ohio; and the abstract of votes, of which a certified copy was taken, by Oliver M. Spencer and George W. Runyan, showed that they had a majority of the votes cast. The question was upon the constitutionality of the act of the legislature of Ohio dividing the county of Hamilton for purposes of representation in the State Legislature. For thirty days the State of Ohio was without a Legislature, in anarchy and confusion, with two conflicting parties contending for pre-eminence; and at the end of thirty days, two gentlemen, still living, honored citizens of Ohio, men of neither the Whig nor the Democratic party, took the responsibility of judging that the certificate of the clerk was the official evidence of the title, and upon it organized that Legislature.

Mr. MATTHEWS. Let me ask you there whether or not both sides were not excluded until after the organization?

Mr. HOADLY. That may be; but the organization——

Mr. MATTHEWS. Mr. Commissioner PAYNE can answer, probably.

Mr. HOADLY. I accept your statement, as you were one of the authors of the illustrious act to which I allude, a partaker of its honors and of its responsibilities; and among the many reasons for which the people of Ohio have to be thankful that you have lived, this is the most conspicuous.

Mr. MATTHEWS. I hope not.

Mr. HOADLY. I will take your statement. At least the abstract did not secure the seats. What did that

act result in ?   As its first result it made it possible
for the black man, who before that time had been an
alien and a vagabond in Ohio, to live on its soil a citizen
of the State.   It made it, in the second place, possible
for him to be heard in a court of justice as a witness
against a white man.   In the third place, it made Salmon
P. Chase Senator of the United States from the State
of Ohio, to begin that illustrious career which ended in
the chief-justiceship of the Supreme Court of the United
States, in which he died.   Every man in Ohio who
joined in this act has been honored by the people of the
State.   George E. Pugh became attorney-general and
senator ; Salmon P. Chase twice governor by the votes
of his then opponents.   I think, as a citizen of Ohio, I
have no reason to be ashamed of the doctrine that the
broad seal of the county of Hamilton is better evidence
of title to office, even though the clerk in issuing it determine against the constitutionality of a statute, than
the abstract of votes copied and certified to by him.

There was no vacancy in the office in Oregon ; I come
back to that.   A vacancy may exist in Oregon when
" *occasioned* by death, refusal to act, neglect to attend,
or otherwise."   My learned friend, Mr. Lawrence, says
the word "otherwise" means every other possible manner
whatsoever.   It is a cardinal rule in the interpretation
of statutes that every word must have its force, and
that words will not be treated as superfluous ; and yet,
by this argument, the learned gentleman has eliminated
all these words, including the word " otherwise," from
the statute.   He defines the word " otherwise " so that
it might as well be obliterated in fact from the law in
which it is written.

And if there shall be any vacancy in the office of elector occasioned by death, refusal to act, neglect to attend, or otherwise—

This means that there are some vacancies which the

electors present may not proceed to fill. It is not " if there shall be *any* vacancy in the office of elector, the electors present shall immediately proceed to fill it," but it is "if there shall be any vacancy *occasioned* by death, refusal to act, neglect to attend, or otherwise." This is the class of vacancies they may fill; not every vacancy. If it had been every vacancy they might fill, then the words, " occasioned by death, refusal to act, neglect to attend, or otherwise," would have been omitted. In order that these words may have their proper force, the word " otherwise " must be construed in its ordinary and normal legal signification, " of other like manner ;" *noscitur a sociis* is the rule. General words are restrained by the fitness of things. We have in the statutes of Ohio a law by which a railroad company may acquire and convey at pleasure all real or personal estate necessary or proper ; and yet the Supreme Court of Ohio, in 10 Ohio State Reports, the case of Coe *v.* The Columbus, Piqua and Indiana Railroad Company, have said that although the language of the statute is general, and they may convey any real estate necessary and proper to be acquired by them, yet they can not convey one foot of the land which is pledged to the maintenance of the public uses for which they are established. They can not convey the track ; they can not convey the right of way except by mortgage ; and that is because the general words are restrained by the fitness of the subject-matter.

"Occasioned by death, refusal to act, neglect to attend, or otherwise," does not mean "occasioned by every possible circumstance on earth." If it did the law would have said so. It means "occasioned by these methods," and not occasioned otherwise except by these methods or the like unto them, in like manner ; death——

Mr. Representative LAWRENCE. Death or something like death.

Mr. HOADLY. Death, or something which comes within the chain of thought which connects these three enumerated classes, consisting of occurrences happening after election. The act of Congress makes the distinction. It says if there is a failure to elect, the Legislature may decide what provision shall be made. If there is a vacancy when the college meets, the Legislature may provide for it. These are all cases of vacancy occurring after the event of the election, and do not contemplate a vacancy which occurs by reason of what I should call the non-filling of the office occasioned by reason of there being a non-election.

Suppose there had been a tie vote. Is that "otherwise?" Does non-election by a tie vote create a vacancy within the meaning of that statute? That tests the question. I say not. Why not? Because "occasioned by death, refusal to act, neglect to attend, or otherwise" are words that can not be dispensed with and necessarily involve the conclusion that there are some methods of occasioning vacancy which are not within the statute. It would have said "if there be any vacancy the electors present may fill it" had it been supposed these words would be interpreted as now claimed. A tie vote involves a vacancy or what may be called by way of courtesy a vacancy. It is a failure to elect which is not contemplated by this statute and not provided for by this statute, and that was the case in the State of Rhode Island of Corliss or might have been. It was alluded to in the decision of the State of Rhode Island. Your honors will find by referring to the brief which we have on file a large number of cases in which the same principle is upheld.

Mr. Commissioner MILLER. What do you make of the words " refusal to act ?"

Mr. HOADLY. An elector who has been elected and refuses to act creates a vacancy. I consider the word "otherwise" to refer to cases which occur after there has been a complete election, just as section 133 of the Revised Statutes of the United States provides. These are all cases coming within this section.

Mr. Commissioner MILLER. You do not think it necessary that he should have accepted or entered on the duties of the office?

Mr. HOADLY. The words, "refusal to act," avoid that difficulty. If it were not for those words and the power of the Legislature to provide in that way, I think the rule would have been otherwise. But where there is an elector in office *de facto*, as Cronin was, another party cannot make a vacancy by refusing to act. The ordinary rule is that in order that a party may resign he must be an incumbent. So Cockburn, chief-justice, in The Queen *v.* Blizzard, Law Reports, 2 Q. B., 55, held; so Sawyer, chief-justice, now Judge of the United States Circuit Court, held, in People *v.* Tilton, 37 California, 617; so it was held in Miller *v.* The Supervisor of Sacramento county, 25 California, 93 ; so in Commonwealth *ex rel.* Broom *v.* Hanley, 9 Pennsylvania State Reports, 513. And it is held in an opinion which I will hand to your honors, received to-day by mail, of the Supreme Court of Missouri, a case printed in the Central Law Journal of St. Louis, volume 4, number 7, on Friday last, page 156, (in accord with the views to which I have alluded), that the office had been once filled, and therefore there was a vacancy ; as they cite with approval the case of The State *v.* Lusk, 18 Missouri, 333, to the effect that if the office had not been filled by the qualification of the officer before his death, there would have been no vacancy.

I come to consider the remaining question in the case. I say that by Oregon Law, as shown by the certificate of the Governor who was obliged to act, as well as by the better opinion, the weight of authority, if not the number of cases in the United States, the mandate to elect is of such paramount authority that the people may not disobey it by voting for a disqualified candidate. My friends on the other side, in order to maintain their proposition, must not only stand upon a violation of the Constitution of the United States by the election of a disqualified person; they must also contend that a plurality may violate the Constitution and prevent an election. That is their proposition ; and by making their candidate, Watts, an officer *de facto* who did not hold the certificate *de facto*, they thus manufacture this violation of the Constitution of the United States by a plurality into a muniment of title to office.

We have several things to consider here : first, the Constitution of the United States says, " thou shalt elect," to the people of Oregon. If I may, without irreverence, borrow the simile, the first great commandment of the gospel of American liberty is " thou shalt elect," and the second is " thou shalt not elect a disqualified candidate." The plurality may elect ; and if the plurality may elect, and electing a disqualified candidate defeats an election, then the plurality may defeat an election. What is more than this, it is perfectly easy for more than three candidates each to receive a majority of votes in the State of Oregon. I will take the liberty to ask your honors' attention to a supposition which fairly illustrates the principle we are considering. Thus we may suppose that in the State of Oregon, where there were three electors to be chosen, 20,000 votes may be cast, divided among six candidates: A. B, and C receive each 9,800 votes; D, E, and F receive 9,700 votes. The remaining 500 votes may be thus distributed: To A, B, and D, 200 votes; to A, C, and D, 200 votes; to B, C, and D, 100 votes. The result will be: For A, 10,200; for B, 10,100; for C, 10,100; and for D, 10,200. Supposing now, that A were disqualified by holding a Federal office, who would be elected, and which rule ought to be adopted? That which rejects A as disqualified, and B and C as not elected, by reason of the votes for them having resulted in a tie, and only D elected; or that which rejects A as disqualified and returns B, C, and D as elected?

This is not very likely to happen at this time, when electors are mere automata to register the wishes of their constituents; but when there shall be three parties again, if that may ever be, and that shall happen which happened in Pennsylvania, that two of them coalesce on the same list of electors, with the intention of dividing the votes of the electors according to the heads of the tickets, as was proposed to be done in Pennsylvania in 1856, this might very easily happen; and yet, according to the proposition of my friends on the other side, the result would be that the man having the highest number of votes was elected though disqualified. Now, the principle, to govern us, must be consistent: First, with the constitutional mandate that the State shall appoint. That is the mandate of the Federal Constitution; it is the mandate of the Revised Statutes; it is the mandate of Oregon. Secondly, with the constitutional inhibition that no person holding an office of trust or profit under the United States shall be appointed. Thirdly, with the rule that a majority vote is not necessary, but a plurality suffices for election. Fourthly, with the possibility to which I have just ad-

dressed my attention. ˙ And, fifthly, to the fact that
upon the views of their work entertained by those who
made the Constitution, the candidates for electors do not
run, like rivals for the office of sheriff, against each
other, but the choice is made by selection of the successful candidates out of the whole list of those named
in that connection.

I have referred your honors to the decision in Maine.
It so happens that in the State of Maine that opinion
of Chief-Justice Mellen, Chief-Justice Weston, and
Judge Parris became crystallized by the legislative department of the State as one of the laws of the State as
early as 1840, and has remained the law of the State of
Maine until now, and my brief refers your honors to
this law of the State of Maine by which ballots cast for
ineligible persons are not to be counted. It is only in
ignorance of this opinion and this legislation that Spear
v. Robinson, 29 Maine, 531 (a decision really directly
in favor of my proposition), and the opinion of the
judges, 38 Maine, 597 (which does not touch the point),
have ever been cited against it.

It is the law of the State of Massachusetts, God bless
her. I have here a book printed by the authority of the
State of Massachusetts, being Reports of Election Cases
in Massachusetts. This book came from the Legislature
of Massachusetts, and in it is a decision in 1849 by a committee, approved by the vote of her Legislature. This
book was compiled by Judge Luther S. Cushing and his
associates, by direction of the Legislature, and printed
by the State for the information of her people and people
beyond her borders, in which it is stated as the law of
Massachusetts that:

There is no reason why a person who votes for an ineligible
candidate should not be put upon the same footing with one who
does not vote at all, as in both cases the parties show a disposition

to prevent an election, and both of them show an unwillingness
to perform their duty by aiding to promote those elections which
are absolutely essential to the existence of the government; for
if every voter refrained wholly from voting, or voted for an ineligible candidate, the result would be the same, no choice; and
although it is true that no penalty is attached by law to a neglect
of this obligation of voting, yet the obligation is not the less plain
for that, and the committee believe it to be a duty too important
to be neglected and too sacred to be trifled with by voting for fic-
titious persons or ineligible candidates.

Maryland spoke in 1794, in the case of Hatcheson
v. Tilden & Bordley, 4 Harris & McHenry, 279; and
in 1865 and 1866 the Legislature of Maryland, acting
once in their legislative capacity, and acting once in
their judicial capacity, followed, in the cause of loyalty
and of reconstruction upon loyal principles, the rule
which Chief-Justice Samuel Chase laid down for their
government. I have the house journal and documents
of the State of Maryland for 1865, which have been
kindly furnished me by a friend in Baltimore in order
that I might present the original authorities to your
honors. In the Constitution of Maryland, as it was in
1865, was the following provision:

If any person has given any aid, comfort, countenance, or support to those engaged in armed hostility to the United States, or
has, by any open deed or word, declared his adhesion to the
cause of the enemies of the United States, or his desire for the
triumph of said enemies of the United States, he is disqualified
from holding any office of honor, profit, or trust, under the laws
of this State.

Hart B. Holton, who had not a majority or plurality
of the votes cast for senator of Howard County in 1865,
contested the seat of Littleton Maclin, who had the
majority of the legal votes of the voters of Howard
County, and on the principles enunciated by Chief-
Justice Chase, because of the disloyalty of Littleton
Maclin, Hart B. Holton gained the seat and sat as a

senator from that county. In 1866, before the house of delegates, acting judicially, George E. Gambrill contested the office of Sprigg Harwood, as clerk of the circuit court of Anne Arundel County, on the ground of constitutional ineligibility, caused by an increase in the profits of this clerkship, while Harwood was a senator from Anne Arundel County in 1865. The committee said that Harwood was ineligible, that it "must be presumed to have been known by every voter," that in a case 'like this it would be highly inexpedient to submit this matter to another election, and on their report the incumbent of the office was ousted and the contestant inducted into the office of clerk of Anne Arundel County.

So in the States of Missouri and Mississippi, by constitutional amendments, introduced and adopted for the purpose of securing the reconstruction of those States in accordance with the loyal sentiment which demanded the maintenance of the Federal Union at all hazards, it was provided that disloyalty should cause such disqualification that votes given for disloyal persons in Mississippi and Missouri should not be cast up or counted as ballots. This principle, springing from our revolutionary fathers and helping the great work of reconstruction, helping to secure the maintenance of the Federal Union and the principles of loyalty to the Federal Union, has so soon as this become so odious to those who maintained and espoused it so recently that by its rejection is to be elected a President of the United States! What is there to the contrary? Six, or eight, or ten *obiter dicta*, and that is the whole of it, and not one of them in conflict with the principle for which we contend. Why, your honors, the presumption *omnia bene et rite esse præsumuntur donec probetur in contrarium*, sustains the action of the governor of Ore-

gon until there shall be produced in evidence something
to show that the governor of Oregon was not justified
in the course which he took. We are justified, then,
in presuming—we need not the evidence which we offer
—that the fact of disqualification existed, and was so
notorious as to work the law of disqualification. Therefore we are within the rule of Furman *v.* Clute, in 50
New York, 451 ; therefore we are within the rule which
has been adopted in the case of Commonwealth *v.* Cluly
in 56 Pennsylvania State Reports, 277 ; so that we are
within the rule which was adopted in the *obiter dicta* to
which I shall refer.

Mr. Commissioner EDMUNDS. Did not the court in
50 New York hold also that every voter must know
what the law was?

Mr. HOADLY. Precisely so ; and it would be a fit-
ting commentary upon the serious character of the sug-
gestions which have been made in disparagement of the
course taken by the governor of the State of Oregon if
it should be held that his course was improper in consequence of the fact that the 15,000 people who voted
for John W. Watts were presumably ignorant of the
Constitution of the United States. Of a lurking
statute hidden in the corners of a statute-book, like the
statute that governed the disqualification of the supervisor of Schenectady, it may well be that the voters
might be ignorant, but of a disqualification inherent in
a constitutional provision which enables the State to
appoint electors no man ought to say that he is ignorant. No man can be heard in any court of law in any
such case to say, I submit, that he is "ignorant."

Three times Indiana has promulgated the principle
which I have suggested. It has been espoused by
Judge Cushing in his book, Sections 177, et seq ; it is
espoused by Grant on Corporations, 208 ; it is the law

of the English and Irish cases, all of which are referred
to in the brief, that a man might as well vote for the
man in the moon, or, as Governor Grover in his decision
says, for Mount Hood, as to vote for a disqualified candidate knowingly ; and what is there to the contrary ?
As I said, the Pennsylvania case concedes that a vote
given with knowlege for an ineligible candidate can not
be counted.   In the cases in California, in the first one,
Melony *v.* Whitman, 10 Cal. 38, the question did not
require or receive decision, for the majority of the court
found that the officer was not ineligible.   In Saunders *v.*
Haynes, 13 Cal. 145, the other case, it is assumed
that a majority of those voting by mistake of law or
·fact happened so to cast their vote.   The case in Wisconsin (State *v.* Giles, 1 Chandl. 112,) which has been
considered the leading case on the other side, is as pure
a piece of *gratis dictum* as ever was pronounced in a court
in this country.   After stating that the officer was not
ineligible, the Court go on to say :

Such being the opinion of the court, it is unnecessary to pass
on the second question whether in the event of the person receiving the highest number of votes being ineligible, the person having the next highest number is elected.

Then, I will not say by the same force with which I
address the pupils in my law school, but by the same
judicial authority that I have the right to express when
I address students in a law school, the court go on,
having decided that it was not their duty to say anything
about it, to expound the law, in order that on future occasions their successors may have the benefit of it, and in
State *v.* Smith, 14 Wisconsin, 497, their successors get
the benefit of it, and adopt it without giving any reasons.
Judge Lumpkin, in Georgia, State *v.* Swearingen, 12
Geo. 23, followed the same wise example, deciding that
no restriction of residence "was imposed on the voters

of the young but rapidly growing town of Oglethorpe in their selection of a suitable person to fill the office of clerk and treasurer." Having decided that there was no such ineligibility, he proceeded to lay down the law of the court *obiter* in these words :

Under no circumstances could we permit the informant to be installed into these appointments.

In Missouri the first case, State *v.* Boal, in 46 Missouri, 528, is in accordance with the views which we maintain.

As regards the votes cast for the defendant, they were nugatory. It was as though no such votes had been cast at the election.

And the case of The State *v.* Vail, 53 Mo. 97, does not withdraw this limitation, but simply confines it to cases of latent disqualification, saying :

It is unnecessary to determine whether it would be the rule in any case of disqualifications, whether patent or latent.

The case in Tennessee, Pearce *v.* Hawkins, 2 Swan, 87, decides that the votes are illegal and void, which is a case, as far as it goes, in our favor. The case in Michigan, People *v.* Molitor, 23 Mich. 341, is disposed of by an admission in pleading; the court say the party admitted his case away in pleading. The case in 21 Louisiana Annual Reports, 289, Fish *v.* Collins, decides, with modesty, I suppose, if there be such an article in the Supreme Court of that State, that it was unnecessary to express an opinion whether the votes cast for a person notoriously known to be ineligible should be rejected or not, as no such allegations were made in the petition. The cases in 18 and 20 Louisiana Annual Reports, 114, State *v.* Gastinel, are to the same effect.

Whatever might have been his rights had he contested the election of the defendant in accordance with law, we are not called upon to say.

The case in Mississippi, Sublett *v.* Bedwell, 47 Miss.
273, is nearest to a case in opposition to the principle
for which I contend, of any in the United States.
There it is said:

> If the majority make choice of a candidate under some per-
> sonal disability disqualifying him from taking and enjoying the
> office, the utmost that can be said of it is that there has been no
> election.

" Personal disability," not the disability of the State
to appoint, but personal disability applicable to the candidate.

In Rhode Island, as is shown by a letter from William Beach Lawrence, of which I have reprinted a large
portion in my brief, the opinion on this proposition is
purely *obiter dictum*, there having been a tie between the
three highest democratic candidates for elector, and,
therefore, the result which was reached by the governor,
that there was no vacancy, a failure to elect being the
necessary result, and not the result produced by the
reasons given by the supreme court.

These are all the cases in the United States. I believe I have referred in my brief to every case within
the borders of this land and of Great Britain, except one
case in Coxe's Reports, page 318, The State *v.* Ander-
son, which went off on the proposition that in *certiorari*
there was a discretion, but the court would not exercise
that discretion to displace a man who was disqualified,
because it would leave the office vacant, and did not allude at all to the question whether there was any antagonist or whether his antagonist received any votes.

And if we look beyond the United States, and assume that the common law of England prevails in Oregon, there is nothing to the contrary of our view.

Now, testing by principle, I say Cronin was elected.
Testing by method, would a *quo warranto* have run in
favor of Watts? Would not the disqualification have

killed his title? Could he by *quo warranto* or *certiorari* or contest have obtained the place? Cronin held it *de facto;* Watts was a postmaster disqualified. Test it now by the rules of method under laws similar to that which we have in Ohio and many of the States in which a *quo warranto* may be supported at the instance of the competing candidate, and pursued, not merely to the ousting of the incumbent, but to the induction of the man who ought to have been successful; and on what principle of law could John W. Watts, who did not hold this commission, have got from any court of justice in this land the title to which he now lays claim? Cronin held the title; Cronin cast the vote; Watts was not elector *de facto*, and it is a question whether he was *de jure.* Ask yourselves, learned judges, whether any one of you sitting in *quo warranto* would have awarded, as against the officer *de facto*, possession of the office to a man whom the Constitution of the country said should not hold it? On principle the mandate to elect was fulfilled by the election of Cronin. If Watts be called elected, the mandate to elect was disobeyed. If Watts be called elected, the mandate not to elect a disqualified person was disobeyed. Tested by method and by the rules which apply in courts of justice, tell me how any lawyer can say that a disqualified candidate can seize an office by any process known to the laws of our country out of the hands of one who holds it *de facto*, even although that one be not elected? He may have a judgment that the office is vacant; that is all he can have, and that is the end of the whole thing as far as he is concerned.

Mr. President and Gentlemen of the Commission: Into your hands, assisted by the enlightened labors of those who are to follow me in argument, I commit this cause. No cause was ever submitted more momentous in its issues or its consequences. It involves the question whether government of the people, by the people, for the people, shall be suspended in the Executive department of these United States for the next four years.

At the election in November last, Samuel J. Tilden and Thomas A. Hendricks received for President and Vice-President of the United States a vast majority of the total popular vote, a majority of the legal popular vote in the States of Louisiana and Florida, and one certificated electoral vote in the State of Oregon. Your sense of duty has prevented your listening to the testimony which would have established their title to the electoral votes of Louisiana and Florida. This was because you possessed no judicial power whatever. Had you been endowed with any portion of the judicial power of the United States, there is no doubt, that, before this time, its exercise would have relieved the people of the United States from the serious apprehension of great danger, of danger that, for four weary years, the choice of the American people shall be frustrated, and a usurper sit in the seat of Washington and Jefferson, of Jackson and of Lincoln.

If you adhere to the principle which has thus far guided your action, this danger will be averted. Without the exercise of judicial power, you can not deprive Tilden and Hendricks of their Oregon vote, or award it to Hayes and Wheeler.

You have been likened unto judges in Israel, and warned not to make your proceedings so intolerably inconvenient that the people should desire a king. The people, whose cause I represent, will never, never, never wish for a king; but I may remind the counsel that it was not because the action of their judges was inconvenient that the people of Israel desired a king, but because their judges "*perverted* judgment."

Conscript Fathers of the American Republic, the flower and crown of the enlightened jurisprudence of pagan Rome were the two maxims, " *Ubi jus, ibi re-medium,*" " *Suum cuique tribuito.*" May it be the happy fortune of our nation and of yourselves, as the expounders of its constitutional powers, not to lessen the force or diminish the universality of their application.

So shall Time, the corroder and consumer of all finite things, pass your work by untouched, and after generations, as they may meet with questions of disputed succession, shall point to and follow it, saying, " Behold the great example of our fathers. In their ways will we walk, for they are the ways of righteous judgment and of peace;" and the arms of them who serve liberty in all the lands shall be strengthened, for they shall know that in monarchies questions of succession are resolved by the sword, in republics by justice.

So shall Art, which keeps in eternal remembrance the realities of things, still delineate Justice with bandaged eyes and open ears, and history shall not record that Justice here, at the expense of her hearing, regained her sight.